A PRAC

GUIDE TO

MINDFUL

LIVING

Five Ways to Restore Presence and Calm
Amidst Challenge and Change

DAVID JOHNSON

A Practical Guide to Mindful Living: Five Ways to Restore Presence and Calm Amidst Challenge and Change

by David Johnson

Published by Samadhi Publications

www.samadhi.org.uk

Front cover photo by David Johnson
Designed by Manuel Orozco Jimenez

ISBN: 978-1-3999-2109-1

Printed in the United Kingdom

First Edition

Contents

Guided Meditation Companion Download

To help you practice, there is a companion audio for each of the nine guided meditations in this book. These are marked with the headphones icon. You can access these audios by scanning the QR code below or visiting: www.samadhi.org.uk/book-meditations

Preface

> *"Find out what really constitutes true well-being and based on this understanding, pursue it."* - The Buddha (Majjhima Nikāya III-230)

Happiness is, I believe, the very defining and driving factor behind the lives of sentient beings. While some of us openly pursue and question the phenomenon that is happiness, its nature, and its causes, we are all - on some level - seeking something better in life.

From an early age, I was fascinated by this question, "how to be happy", the mind and mental health, and as I grew up, I saw so much suffering around me, and this drove me to want to help. However, in order to be able to help, I had to first find the solution to mental suffering and then see where I could help people find the freedom they sought.

Naturally, living in modern Europe, with no real education in the nature of the mind, the first place I turned to was medicine and science - so I thought to pursue psychology and psychiatry. After a failed application to study medicine at university, but with a continued desire to help people and find answers, I took a job as a support worker in a local psychiatric hospital. It wasn't long before I saw a huge number of people coming into this hospital not with severe mental illness but with generalised low mood and anxiety disorders caused or exacerbated by the struggles and challenges of daily life. There were many people struggling with trauma, addiction, and an inability to regulate their emotions in a healthy way. For these people, I was surprised to see an emphasis on pharmaceutical intervention, which focused primarily on suppressing symptoms, not on what I thought was important: getting to the root cause of their symptoms and doing the work to eradicate it. This was for various reasons, including not surprisingly, a lack of adequate funding. Not entirely agreeing with this approach, I moved to a bigger city, to a health trust which had more funding and seemed more progressive and cutting edge. Here, I felt I would get a better view of how forward thinkers were applying the latest knowledge and insights about the mind and mental ill health. I hopped between various jobs and learned a lot about psychiatry, psychology, and community health, and while there was great work being done for those with severe mental illness, for various reasons, I found that there was still a lack of what I felt was truly important: people coming into the service with low mood, anxiety, and emotional or behavioural difficulties, receiving a treatment which improved their mental health and wellbeing and healed them of their afflictions, and leaving out the other side. "Revolving door" cases were the norm, as were cynical staff, a lack of adequate psychological or therapeutic input, and a suppression of symptoms via pharmaceuticals. This is not to say that medication does not play a role in recovery, and for many it is vital, but we should be clear that it treats symptoms only and is not a cure.

On a daily basis, I was witnessing intense mental suffering from those in our care, and around the same time, my parents were struggling with their physical and mental health too, and we had several deaths in our immediate family. News and media felt particularly bleak, with an overwhelming number of stories talking about death, destruction, famine and war, and social media was rife with fear and hate. With so much suffering around me and with no answers or wisdom to turn what I was experiencing into compassion or any useful emotion, I fell into grief and depression.

It was at my lowest point looking for an "out" that I was very fortunate to discover meditation and the teachings of the Buddha. Here was a methodical approach, a way of looking closely at and investigating the very nature of human experience, our mind, our pursuit of happiness, and our seemingly unceasing experience of suffering. Based on rationalism, here was a structured sequence of practices that were analytical, and which had correlations to modern quantitative science. There was no dogma, no belief system to subscribe to; simply a community of people asking the right questions about mind and mental suffering, investigating hypotheses, and testing them against their experience in a very straightforward way.

From my upbringing, I had an aversion to religion, and Buddhism, to me, was just another one. I was surprised to find that the teachings I was receiving were more suited to the categories of philosophy, psychology, and science. It was later pointed out to me that these three categories – science, philosophy, and religion – are western categories, and this explains why Buddhism doesn't seem to fit into any one of them exclusively.

It's safe to say that it has been a love affair ever since. I feel very fortunate to have met many skilled Dharma teachers and have enjoyed studying and practising under their guidance. I can truly say that the teachings I will share with you in this book have transformed my life, and I've witnessed them change the lives of others. I feel very humbled and glad to have the opportunity to illuminate and share this truly transformative Dharma of which I am so grateful.

In writing this book on the topics of meditation and Buddhism, I do not claim to be a learned scholar, a spiritual guide or guru, or someone worth any particular acclaim – I simply wish to share these teachings from the perspective of someone who has struggled with unhappiness as so many do. Equally, in the spirit and in the manner that the Buddha taught, I do not claim that anything contained in this book is to be believed simply on the basis of it appearing in a book or on the basis of it having been said by some scholars, lamas, yogis, and contemplatives of the past. Instead, we should address the material in this book in the manner of "*ehipassiko*", a Pali word that simply means to "come and see". Blind faith is strongly discouraged, and I would encourage you to instead strive to experience and discover the benefits of the practices introduced in this book through your own direct experience and investigation.

Acknowledgements

I would like to say a special thank you to all my kind teachers, especially my root Lama, B. Alan Wallace, also to my partner, Manu, for his unwavering support and generosity, and to my students and friends from around the world for their dedication to practice, which has inspired me to write this book.

The teachings and tools shared here in this book came together following an online course held in the early part of 2021 entitled "Mindful Living". The course aimed to introduce and explore five simple ways to live more mindfully and, in doing so, uncover our natural capacity for genuine happiness and wellbeing. It was suggested that turning those teachings into a practical guide such as this would be beneficial to others. This book is thanks to the kindness of friends, students, and volunteers. Firstly, Lucy Hughes volunteered to carefully transcribe the entire five week course. I then edited and added to these transcripts over the course of a year, and this book began to take form. Following this, I was very fortunate that Rebecca Dibben volunteered her time as a professional proofreader and editor. Her wonderful work checking and polishing the book has made the book you have here today a much smoother and clearer read. I am grateful to everyone who has contributed.

Each of the five ways to live more mindfully has its own section. Intertwined with these five ways are interludes of meditation practices and meditation skills training. These interludes build progressively, providing some of the theory and tools behind concentration meditation, or *shamatha*, and how to overcome the issues of sleepiness and distraction in meditation. These are explored through a mixture of theory, practice, and guided meditations.

Primarily, I want to provide you with what I have found to be the most useful, the most practical, down-to-earth practices and mindset shifts that will make an impact on your life and your daily experience as soon as you practice them.

The five different ways that we can bring mindfulness into our daily life that we will explore are:

1. Cultivating mindfulness through a daily meditation practice.

2. Leading a meaningful and deliberate life by being mindful of our choices and making choices that lead to genuine wellbeing and happiness.

3. Spending less time living in our imagination and more time living in the present moment.

4. Mindful activities – such as mindful walking, mindful eating, or mindful drinking.

5. Mindfulness of the mind, thoughts, and emotions, and recognising their not-self nature.

The teachings which I will share in this book come from several sources. Primarily, they are in accordance with the teachings of the Buddha, as I have received and understood them from my teachers over the years. Secondly, there are influences from both my teacher, world-renowned Tibetan Buddhist scholar B. Alan Wallace, and the Mindfulness-Based Stress Reduction (MBSR) programme. Thirdly, all of these discussions are influenced by my practical experience of these methods in my life and reports from my students. There is nothing in this book that I can say is truly "mine" in any way, rather it is a collection of practices and teachings that I have inherited. Having said that, any errors that may be found are completely my own.

I have done my best to ensure the contents of this book are clear, accurate, and practical, and that my motivation while writing has been inspired by compassion. I hope the teachings in this book will prove as beneficial to you as they have to me.

Dedication

May all beings find happiness and the causes of happiness.

May all beings find freedom from suffering and the causes of suffering.

May all beings be safe and protected, free from inner and outer harm.

May all beings find peace in an uncertain world.

Introduction

Mindless Living

Mindfulness is becoming increasingly popular and for a good reason – with many benefits to be achieved in our mental, physical, and emotional wellbeing. But with so many apps, courses, and videos out there and so many different approaches, it can be unclear precisely what mindfulness is or how and why we want to apply it to our daily lives.

The fact is that many of us in this world are living quite mindlessly, not mindfully. Sometimes it can feel like we're wandering from one day to the next, fighting fires, dealing with the latest hurdle, responding to whatever's going on in our life, without end, and without a meaningful purpose. We do our usual routine of breakfast, commute, work, TV, music, and so on, then we go to bed, and we may not even take notice as the days go by. We can look back, and it seems that so much happened automatically, like we were physically present but mentally elsewhere.

Because of this, we might feel like we're not living as purposefully as we'd like to, as the days, weeks, and months pass by, we're not sure what happened or what we achieved, and we're not sure if we've moved any closer to the life we want to live. As I write this book in 2021, we're coming out of the latest series of lockdowns. It seems as though many people have put their life on hold for a long time because they've had to stay at home without much freedom. Many people seem to be waiting for their life to start up again, and that's quite a dangerous way to think because if we have put our life on hold, then we're not making the most of the moment that we have now.

Right now, this very moment as you read this book, is your life right now, for better or worse. Whether we're in a lockdown or we feel we're being held back by something else in life, it's a shame if we put our life on hold, ourselves on hold, and the things we want to achieve on hold because we feel our life is on pause. Many of us spend a great deal of our life waiting. We think of our workday in terms of getting to the end of it; we think of our week in terms of what we have planned ahead and the weekend. When we're driving or doing our commute, we think in terms of the hours or minutes left until we reach our destination. We count down the weeks and days until our holiday, and then when our holiday begins, we count the days left and plan out as many activities as we can. We're always stressing and waiting for that next moment. In this way, we miss out on the subtle joy there is to be found in the present moment. We treat our life as if it is all about the destination and not about the journey. But life can be seen as a piece of music, where the goal is not to get to the end of the song but to savour and enjoy each beautiful moment. After all, life unfolds in moments, and the joys available in this life are experienced in this moment and not the next.

With the break-neck pace that life can have, we may find that we've been experiencing a lot of excess stress, mood swings, and tiredness; perhaps we feel low on energy, or we spend a lot of time worrying or overthinking. These, by and large, could be seen as symptoms of mindless living and a mind that is un-balanced and unhealthy.

But this is not something we've consciously caused or something to feel guilty about. It is a wide-spread experience that modern life has exacerbated. Generation on generation, in the pursuit of making things more convenient, more entertaining, faster, and easier, we have made our lives more complex, with a relentless pace that we struggle to keep up with, with more stimulus, more noise, and more turbulence. Because of this, as we try to keep up, life naturally lends itself to living more unconsciously – we have no time and no patience for slowing down. It's a fast-paced, stimulus-driven way of life – we're always contactable, always "on", and there's pressure to get ahead and progress. The result of all of this is that as a society, we're becoming more impatient, more dissatisfied, more unhappy, and more mindless than ever before. We're putting more and more of our day-to-day tasks on automate because we're too busy worrying and consumed in what's coming next: the planning, the organising, the remembering, the upcoming tasks, the deadlines, that meeting, what I need to do tomorrow, and next week. While we are physically present, our mind is elsewhere. Our mind is thinking about other things that we have to do, other places we should be, things we need to sort out. Perhaps even as we wake up in the morning, we're not fully aware that we have woken up because our mind has already gone to think about the tasks that we need to sort out, the things that we need to organise, the assignments we have, the deadlines that are coming up. As we're physically just getting out of bed, the mind is already away; it's at work already; it's worrying about the things we need to do.

This creates a disconnect between our physical body and our mind. There's a disconnect between what is actually happening – right here, right now – and the focus of our awareness. Even as we go for a hike, we may not enjoy the sounds and sights of nature because our mind is replaying memories, a recent argument with our partner, a worrying conversation with a friend. As we sit at our desk, we're not fully productive because we're daydreaming about winning the lottery and never having to work again. As we drive around, our mind might be still in the office: brainstorming, composing emails, and organising.

In summary, I think it's safe to say that many of us are obsessively distracted from the moment we get up to the moment we go to bed. From both our own first-person experience and scientific research, we see that this is an unhealthy way to live and doesn't bring about happiness and a sense of wellbeing.

Harvard researchers concluded that about 50% of the time, we're actually distracted from what we're doing. I suspect that figure is probably a lot higher. However, even if the 50% figure is accurate, then we have to admit that an entire half of our life is spent not being present with what we're doing but instead worrying about the past or future. Factor in how much time we spend asleep, and we come to a remarkable conclusion about an element of essential self-care that we've been neglecting. Interestingly, research has also highlighted the connection between happiness and being present. People who are mindfully present and actively concentrating on what they were doing report higher happiness levels and higher levels of feeling like their life has meaning and purpose.

This is one of many pieces of research and evidence that confirms what the Buddha knew 2,600+ years ago: that mindfulness is a crucial component of living our best, happiest, most fulfilled life.

Inner Transformation Through Mindfulness

I first came across mindfulness when I was working in mental health services in the NHS. I was trained in a trial programme designed to help people reclaim their mental wellbeing and discover a renewed sense of enthusiasm and joy for life as they recovered from mental ill health. This programme combined Cognitive Behavioural Therapy (CBT) techniques, insights from psychology, and mindfulness tools. I took the time to try the mindfulness practices we were taught and found they were quite beneficial for my wellbeing, and they seemed to impact those in my care positively. It wasn't until my own journey and struggles with mental ill health that my exploration of mindfulness came alive, and I ended up at its root: Buddhism. Buddhism offered a logical and natural exploration of the mind, mental wellbeing, and the broader question of human suffering in general. There was no dogma to believe in, blind faith was discouraged, and everyone encouraged testing out the practices, tools, and theories for myself. As I studied and practised what I was taught, I found an inner transformation was taking place. I became a more peaceful and positive person and began to access an inner wellbeing that could support me no matter my external circumstances. My relationships became more harmonious, and my work became more manageable. Problems became easier to deal with and less catastrophic. This wasn't because my outer world was changing; it was because my inner world was changing. I didn't need to change my job, relationship, or living arrangements, but a remarkable thing happened: my inner transformation led to an outer transformation of the reality I was inhabiting. As my perception became more realistic and I stopped fighting the world I was in, a natural joy began to emerge, and the way I viewed things changed. Although I was not cured of all challenging emotions and unhappiness, I was becoming more balanced, and life had become noticeably easier. I was convinced with my small progress that this was a path worth following. The Buddha is often quoted as saying: "In the past, monks, and also now, I teach suffering and the cessation of suffering." This is the whole purpose of Buddhist teachings, to provide us with a path towards greater happiness and reduced suffering.

The Pursuit of Happiness

When it comes to approaching the topic of our pursuit of happiness, Buddhism's approach is very methodical and starts not in some far away philosophy but right where we are and our current experience.

When we investigate the way we interact with the world, other people, and our environment, our primary motivators become apparent. It's easy to see that we have a preference for physical and mental comfort – what we can broadly call happiness (in Sanskrit, *sukha*). From the biggest decisions in our day, such as to put on a jacket when it's cold or to take it off when it's warm, to the bigger decisions such as where to live, whom to spend time with, or what to do with our life – it's all in the pursuit of moving towards pleasurable experiences.

The flip side of this is that we're avoiding any displeasurable experience, or discomfort – what we can broadly call suffering (in Sanskrit, *dukkha*). Every action we take, every decision we make, and every decision any sentient being makes is based on this preference: to experience pleasure, or happiness, and to avoid any discomfort and any displeasure, or suffering.

The question, then, naturally arises, if we do all have this preference, and we've spent our entire lives from the moment we were born – think rejecting the food we didn't like and screaming when we needed a nappy change – then why have we not found lasting, genuine happiness and freedom from suffering? Why is it that we still have to deal with emotions like jealousy, frustration, anger, sadness, anxiety, and we still have to deal with challenging situations and experiences?

One fruitful hypothesis by the Buddha is that our recipe is faulty. Like having a recipe for cookies that always results in an over-baked, salty hockey puck, which we are continuously repeating over and over, serving to ourselves and our loved ones.

There has been an incredible material progression in our modern world. The advances in science, medicine, and technology are truly outstanding. The things we can achieve, and the things with which we can access on our laptops and phones are awe-inspiring. These advances were all in the pursuit of progress – of improving, making things more convenient, easier, better, faster.

Despite this material progress, the research shows that there is no corresponding progress in human happiness. In fact, studies show that since the 1940s, there has been a dramatic divergence between real income (after taxes and inflation) and life satisfaction (Diener and Seligman, 2004), with life satisfaction almost remaining flat while income has increased considerably. And indeed, when we consider measures of ill health, such as depression rates and anxiety rates, we see that they have increased significantly during this same period (Twenge, 2002).

This shows that while there is an undeniable value in wellbeing and satisfaction that comes from the material world (such as having a home, access to food, water, clothing, and education), we see that the happiness gained from these sources has its limitations, and after a certain point, the level of happiness does not continue to grow.

It has been identified by many contemplatives, philosophers, and thinkers from the west and east that generally, there are two types of happiness and wellbeing that we can experience: hedonic (in Sanskrit, *laukika-sukha*) and genuine (in Sanskrit, *samyak-sukha*).

Hedonic Happiness

The Buddha taught that there are four types of hedonic happiness, that have a direct impact on our ability to be happy and be well in mind and body. To quote from the Pali Canon:

> *"There are these four kinds of happiness to be won by a householder who enjoys sense pleasures from time to time and when occasion offers. What four? The happiness of ownership, the happiness of wealth, the happiness of freedom from debt, and the happiness of a clear conscience."* – The Buddha (Aṅguttara Nikāya II-68)

The happiness of ownership

By the happiness of ownership, the Buddha is refer-ring to having enough – having enough food, cloth-ing, shelter. It is universally recognised that, generally, without these things, it's harder to be happy. This is a type of hedonia which for most, makes us happier, calmer people. Having said that, the key takeaway from this is that having 10 times or 20 times the amount of food, clothing, or shelter you need does not make you any happier, as demonstrated by the research mentioned above and by our own experi-ence.

The happiness of wealth

The second type of happiness cited here is the hap-piness of wealth. Here the Buddha is referring to hav-ing that bit more than you need – the financial free-dom to be able to see friends, to have holidays, to give to charity, without worrying about whether it will affect your ability to afford the basic necessities. Again, as with the first, this type of happiness also has a ceiling, in which any more will not bring about more happiness or wellbeing.

The happiness of freedom from debt

The third type of happiness is the happiness of freedom from debt. This is the type of debt that would get you into prison, the kind of debt you could never repay and can't escape.

The happiness of blamelessness (or clear conscience)

The fourth type of happiness is the happiness of blamelessness or clear conscience. This is about not experiencing the poison of guilt. It is knowing we're living a life that is not causing harm to others and that we're not in conflict with others. It is good to recognise our errors, feel remorse, and rectify them, but to be struck with guilt and grief over them, will put blockers in the way of your ability to be happy.

It is not difficult to recognise what role the four kinds of happiness play in our life, how they have affected our ability to be happy in the past, and how they affect it now. Furthermore, it is of great importance that we recognise how much of our time and energy we spend on number one and number two; the happiness of ownership and the happiness of wealth. We should question whether we recognise its limitations to make us happy.

The faults of hedonic pleasure

Hedonic happiness is about what we get from the world. By its very nature, it is subject to the following six faults, which I will explain in this chapter:

1. It never truly satisfies.
2. It only lasts as long as the stimulus is present.
3. It can turn into suffering.
4. It can't be enjoyed with an uncontrolled mind.
5. It is unreliable and unable to be controlled.
6. It is subject to impermanence.

It never truly satisfies

We normally think that being happy is about acquiring the good things in life – a good job, a good partner, a good house, a good car, and so on. We think that by getting all these things arranged perfectly "then I'll be happy". Thinking back on our life we may recognise that we have spent a lot of time, energy, and money on our pursuit of the good things in life. Our next question then, naturally, should be, "what do I have to show for it"?

At each milestone and with each new partner, house, or car, did we find the happiness and contentment that we were seeking? Or did it, in fact, satisfy for a while, but then become dull, or show its faults, or break, or leave? When we first meet a new partner, things are exciting, they are very loving and kind, and they are perfect for us – we don't really see any faults or issues, and if there are any, we can easily overlook them because this person is perfect. Over time, as the honeymoon period cools off, the cracks start to show, and we start to see all the negative sides that we thought weren't there or weren't such a big deal. So, then we either become bored but stick with them or start looking for someone new. The same happens with our material possessions – the latest phone with an all-new amazing camera, the best camera, the best screen – how long is it before there is a new best and our old best becomes boring and no longer fulfils our desire?

This is what is meant by hedonic pleasure never truly satisfying: it is a dog chasing a metal bunny, a treadmill that never ends. If our desires are fulfilled, and we experience some pleasure or happiness as a result, it's not long before it's not enough, we become bored, and we look to the next thing.

It only lasts as long as the stimulus is present

Hedonic pleasure is stimulus-based and, therefore, only lasts as long as the stimulus is present. Pleasure or happiness that is experienced as a result of a good meal, time with old friends, or a walk on the beach, will only last for as long as the event lasts. Take the stimulus away, the pleasure and the good feeling stops. We all know that saying that "all good things must come to an end", well, they do, and if our recipe for happiness is to have consistent pleasurable stimulus 24/7, then we all know why this won't work.

It can turn into suffering

All of the examples mentioned above – a good meal, time with old friends, a walk on the beach – can all turn into suffering. If a good meal was in the nature of happiness, then it would follow that the more of it I got, the happier I would become. However, we know from experience that there comes a point in which there is too much pizza, too much ice cream, too much of our friends, and too much sand, wind, or rain. Thus, hedonic pleasure can turn into suffering. If it truly was in the nature of happiness, then happiness would be its only nature.

It can't be enjoyed with an uncontrolled mind

We perceive material possession and enjoyable external events to be causes of happiness and pleasure from their own side, almost as if our mind plays no role. For example, some say, "walking on the beach makes me happy". In reality, whatever pleasurable or joyful feeling we get from the external world comes from the side of the mind. We can see from our own experience that when we are upset or angry, our possessions can mean nothing to us; we may throw them against a wall or break them. When our mind is disturbed, our collection of "good" things isn't able to protect us and provide us with the comfort we seek. If we are upset, angry, or stressed, then our walk on the beach becomes full of faults – it's too windy, too hot, too cold, too wet, too noisy, and so on. If the walk on the beach truly was a cause of happiness from its own side, and our mind had no role to play, then everyone would enjoy this experience and immediately become happy, no matter how they felt previously or what mind they brought with them. We know this not to be true. If we have a sour mind, even the most enjoyable experiences can be ruined, and not everyone enjoys a walk on the beach!

It is unreliable and unable to be controlled

In this world, nothing is truly under our control. For example, we may have the perfect partner, but can we control their every movement and ensure their behaviour and actions lead to our happiness? Can we stop them from disappointing us? Or, despite our every effort, do they still leave their dirty socks on the floor and dirty cups next to the sink? Try as we may, can we promise to have a good day tomorrow, free of problems? Or are we, in fact, at the mercy of the universe, where good and bad things are all possible? Happiness and pleasure by way of the external world are unreliable and unable to be sufficiently controlled – it is impossible to assume that we can control everything outside of us, fulfil all our desires, and avoid any upsetting situations.

It is subject to impermanence

"Everything that has a beginning has an ending. Make your peace with that, and all will be well." – Jack Kornfield

In this famous quote, Jack Kornfield was highlighting the truth of impermanence – that everything is in a constant state of flux – our bodies, our possessions, the world around us, and all who inhabit it. All of these things, including the things which we perceive make us happy, are subject to wear and tear and an eventual ceasing to be. Research suggests that even our bodies are completely replaced on a cellular level every 7-10 years. Emotionally and physically, we are constantly changing, and so are our partners. Our car, our phone, our home, will all start to fall apart and will eventually break or cease to be. Because everything is in a state of flux, its ability to continue to trigger happiness or pleasure in us is also in a state of flux.

This is what is meant by the hypothesis of the faulty recipe, what psychologists call the "hedonic treadmill". As we can see from our above analysis of hedonic happiness, while some hedonic pleasure has an essential role to play in our general wellbeing (it is, of course, much more difficult to have a peaceful and happy mind if you have no food, shelter, clothing, or education), to experience a more lasting, genuine, and deeper level of mental wellbeing and happiness, we must look elsewhere. This does not mean that we should now throw away all our possessions, give away our clothes and live in a cave wearing nothing but a loincloth. This is, instead, about recognising the limitations that external pleasures have in our quest to find lasting, genuine happiness. The possessions we have and the experiences we enjoy are not the problem. The problem is the control that these things currently have over us. We will discuss the difference between these two types of happiness and how to cultivate genuine lasting happiness in more detail in the chapter on *Leading a Meaningful and Deliberate Life*.

Our first step towards finding some sort of freedom from the ups and downs of daily life is to relinquish the control the external world has over us and our emotions. The key to doing this is learning to live mindfully.

Mindful Living

What is Mindfulness?

The classic Buddhist meaning behind mindfulness is simply "bearing in mind" the object of attention – the state of not forgetting, of not being distracted, and not floating. However, the modern vipassana approach and the approach of the MBSR programme define mindfulness as a "non-discriminating, moment to moment, bare awareness of whatever arises." These two definitions can appear on the surface to be conflicting, but I believe they are very compatible.

If we look at this first one, mindfulness being a translation of the Sanskrit *smrti* or the Pali *sati*, this term literally means "to bear in mind", or "to recollect" something. This definition of mindfulness fits very closely with how we use the phrases "be mindful" and "bear in mind" in our everyday language. We might see a sign that says "mind your head" which means you need to bear your head in mind because you might hit it! It means "remember your head"! If somebody says, "be mindful that we agreed to do that thing later" that means you need to bear in mind, remember, or recollect that you agreed to do something. So, mindfulness, as a translation, of *sati* or *smrti*, is very good. To quote B. Alan Wallace:

> "The primary meaning of sati, is recollection, non-forgetfulness. This includes retrospective memory of things in the past, prospectively remembering to do something in the future, and present-centered recollection in the sense of maintaining unwavering attention to a present reality. The opposite of mindfulness is forgetfulness, so mindfulness applied to the breath, for instance, involves continuous, unwavering attention to the respiration."

The Buddhist tradition gives us three types: mindfulness of something from the past, mindfulness of the present, and mindfulness of something relevant in the future. Retrospective mindfulness is, for example, remembering where we live, remembering how to sit when we meditate, or remembering what we're supposed to be doing when we are meditating. Here we recall some important information from the past, and we bear it in mind. The second type, present-centred mindfulness, is maintaining your attention on this book, or attending to how the book feels in your hand. This type is about being fully attentive to the task at hand and what is happening in the present moment. The third type, prospective mindfulness, is remembering something in advance, such as when we need to do something in the future – for example, remembering that when we're on our way home, we need to pick up bread. When we're mindful of that fact, we don't spend the whole day repeating the thought, "I need to pick up bread, I need to pick up bread, I need to pick up bread", like a mantra. We are aware that we need to pick up bread, but it's prospective mindfulness – bearing in mind something important for the future.

The definition of mindfulness that we see from the vipassana movement and MBSR programme (the "non-discriminating, moment to moment, bare awareness") is one that has attracted much debate, with B. Alan Wallace concluding that, from a Buddhist perspective, their focus of bare attention corresponds much more closely to the Pali term *manasikara*, which is commonly translated as "attention" or "mental engagement" rather than the Pali term *sati* which has a much richer meaning. *Sati* is closely engaged with the chosen object of attention, it enables us to maintain our attention without forgetfulness, it holds the attention firmly to its chosen object and it has a discerning quality. Bare attention on the other hand is the bare cognising of an object, before one begins to recognise, identify, and conceptualise.

Despite these differences, the practice of mindfulness as a non-judgemental awareness of what is arising in the present moment has been proven to be a beneficial practice to engage in. Mindfulness grounds us and gives us relief from repetitive and unhelpful thoughts. There is a lot of research that demonstrates how being mindful in this way helps us reduce stress, anxiety, and cultivate higher degrees of mental wellbeing. For this reason, I think these two definitions are very compatible.

Now, with my primary background being in the Buddhist tradition, I use the first definition, and for the purpose of this book, when I say mindfulness, I'm going to be referring to *sati*, bearing in mind without forgetfulness.

The definitions have been given here for the benefit of background theory, but won't really be given much attention from here. Instead, our focus will be: what is the practice? What can it do for my life? How do I use it?

Why Live Mindfully?

By living mindfully, we'll be practising an effective way of taking control of our life and enhancing our emotional and mental health. Essentially, that is what mindful living unlocks for us. It helps us manage life's stresses and handle what's happening in our lives effectively, to be at peace with ourselves, and be at peace with our surroundings.

When we practise mindful living, we're trying our very best to live life moment by moment, thus becoming more aware of ourselves and more aware of the reality that we're currently experiencing. A teacher of mine once said that we take life too seriously in many ways, almost like a kid who has built a sandcastle that starts to get washed away. We cling tightly to our sandcastles and reject the waves of life. We're very attached to things being the way we think they should be and reject what is actually happening before us. When we're in a difficult situation, it feels as if that situation will be here forever. It's dire, awful, and very worrying. We reject it and feel that we do not have the strength to overcome it. As we view things in this way and get fixated on them, we do not see the bigger picture. We do not see that waves are what naturally happens to sandcastles on the beach.

By thinking on some level that our problems are fixed and stable and worrying about how things will turn out and why we need things to change, we're not living moment to moment with whatever is coming up and dealing with the reality we're currently experiencing. We're fixated on the rejecting, and we're fixated on the next moment.

The truth is that the vast majority of the time, the very moment we live in is good; it's peaceful, calm, and OK. A lot of the suffering that we experience is when we're worrying about something that will happen in the future (or that we believe might happen). For example, a 15 minute meeting that we're dreading. We can cause ourselves days of trauma and stress worrying about how that's going to go: what's going to be said, how we're going to say it, what we'll do if they respond this way, rehearsing our arguments and responses. We may struggle with this worry all evening, the following morning, and during the journey to the meeting. We then get to that meeting, and only the first two minutes are demanding, and then it's over! One week later, those two minutes won't matter. One month later, we probably won't even remember it. One year later, five years, 10 years, we definitely won't remember it. Despite this, we waste valuable moments of our life worrying about two minutes. If we could look back and see the many hours, days, and weeks that we've spent worrying, would we be glad of how we used our time?

The vast majority of moments of any given 24 hour period are actually good. If we open ourselves up to them and let go of our worries, we see that in this moment, everything is OK, nothing is going wrong, and we can be at peace. We know this from our own experience – we all experience some calmer, quieter parts of our day, perhaps when we go for a nice walk, or when making a coffee, or doing some crafts. These moments of calm are enjoyable. Some people have daily routines where they are quiet, and those moments we love and cherish! In those moments, we're not flustered or caught up in the worries of the day, but we're fully present with what we're doing. In our attentive presence lies a tranquillity of body and mind, and out of that tranquillity emerges natural healing, balancing, and relaxation. All of this is brought about because we let go of the distraction, rumination, and worrying about the past and future.

Mindful living means to be more aware of ourselves and the reality that we're currently experiencing. The practices that we're exploring help us bring more attention to different areas of our life, and bring more peace and calm, healing us of our chronic distractibility and mental imbalances.

People who live mindfully tend to be very comfortable in themselves. However high or low their material achievements are, however much or little they have, they tend to be very much at peace with themselves. They have the manner of being in control of the things around them without actually showing any outward action of controlling them. They're not dashing around hurriedly sorting this or that. They just seem to be more organised, calmer, and have better concentration. This all comes with being more present with ourselves, being more present with reality, and having unity of mind and body. Our mind and body are utterly entwined, connected like the two wings of a bird. This disconnect that can occur between them is very unhealthy for our wellbeing. By practising mindful living, we cultivate unity of body and mind and an awareness of how unconscious thoughts, feelings, and behaviours can actually undermine our emotional, physical, and spiritual health.

In essence, the practices outlined here will help us to get ourselves unstuck and help us get back in touch with our own wisdom, our own vitality, and our own inner nature, which is calm, peaceful, and content. It will allow us to take charge of our life, improve the quality of our life, including our relationships with others, and most fundamentally, our relationship with ourselves.

Present-Centring

I will now introduce a practice designed to help us bring ourselves back into the present moment when we have become lost in worries of the future or resentments of the past. Present-centring is a skill that we need to develop in order to live mindfully and purposefully. Without this essential skill, we'll struggle to engage in many of the other practices introduced in this book.

It is OK if chronic distractibility is our norm; many of us have poor attention skills, and it is very natural to spend most of our day thinking about the future, the past, or worrying about other things. In Buddhism, this is described as the *monkey mind* because just like a monkey jumping from branch to branch, our uncontrolled mind jumps around from one object to another uncontrollably and without end. Even during our meals, instead of being present and enjoying the tastes and textures in front of us, we're often elsewhere, chatting away or watching TV in the background. We get to the end of our meal and can only really remember that it was good or bad, but not much more.

So, this practice of present-centring is essential and the key with which we unlock mindful living. This particular practice is something you can do anytime and anywhere. For now, I encourage you to take your time with it, but once you're familiar with it, it will be something that you can do relatively quickly anytime you need it. When you do this present-centring practice in your daily life, you won't need to assume a specific meditation posture. You could engage in the practice while waiting in the line at the supermarket or while sitting with your eyes open at your desk in the office. For now, however, as you practice in conjunction with reading this book, I would like for you to adopt an appropriate meditation posture to experience the benefits of doing so.

For most of the meditations in this book, you can choose between either sitting upright or lying down. A walking meditation is described later in the chapter on *Mindful Activities* and standing meditation can be an interesting one to experiment with. These are the four meditation postures the Buddha recommended we try out: walking, sitting, standing, and lying down. I will let you know if there's a particular posture that is recommended before each practice. When we do the seated posture, try your best to follow the *seven-point meditation posture*.

The Seven-Point Meditation Posture

The seven points are:

1. Legs.
2. Hands & Arms.

3. Back.
4. Jaw & Tongue.
5. Head.
6. Eyes.
7. Shoulders.

Your legs – we have several options for our legs. The first is the classic vajra posture or full lotus (a), and that's where you have both feet placed, sole upwards, on the opposite thigh. This posture can be challenging, and I would recommend you only do this if you are very flexible or have approached this posture through another practice such as yoga. The vajra posture gives the best support to the body but is not essential, and for most of us, it's a posture you would have to work your way up to in order not to damage your knees. If you're not very flexible and not naturally able to get into that position, then the half lotus (b), where the left foot is on the floor underneath the right leg and the right foot is on top of the left thigh, is also very beneficial. If this is also challenging, simply crossing your legs with both feet on the floor in the Burmese posture (c) is another option that, for many, is quite comfortable. There will be some trial and error here, which every new meditator goes through, as some ways will lead to a dead leg, or pins and needles, as you figure out the best way of crossing your legs. A firm and high cushion underneath you can be quite beneficial in helping you keep your back straight and aiding you to sit longer without cutting the circulation to your legs. You could also try using a meditation stool or you can even practice meditation by simply sitting in a chair (d) as well, like a dining chair or an office chair. In a chair, it's helpful to place your feet flat on the ground if possible, and have your hips slightly higher than your knees. There are so many different ways that you can position your legs, and I recommend that you try out different ones to see which one gives you the least discomfort and which one allows you to be quite still and relaxed, which are essential qualities of meditation.

Your hands and arms - the second point of the seven-point posture is your hands and arms. Classically, your arms should be relaxed, not pressed against your body but a few inches away to allow air circulation. For your hands, you can choose the traditional mudra of meditative equipoise, or *dhyana mudra*, which is your right hand on top of your left with your thumbs gently touching, and you rest that in your lap about two inches below the navel. Other people prefer to put their hands on their knees, and other people just rest them wherever they fall. Your arms should not be tight against your body but allow them to be slightly apart. A classic instruction I've heard is to hold your arms out slightly as if you were holding an egg in your armpit. I'm not sure why you would want to hold an egg in your armpit, but it's a helpful instruction! You might find that having your hands and arms in a specific place, like described above, helps you maintain the third point: the back.

Your back - your back is the most important point. The spine should be straight, not rigidly so, and not tense, but it should be upright in a relaxed way. Keeping the back straight can be challenging at first, but a firm cushion and appropriate posture for the legs and arms will help you maintain a straight back. Having a straight back allows the energies to flow in the body and helps you remain focused and keep alert and awake. If you slump in any direction or have a curved back, you run the risk of becoming dull and sleepy. It's also been reported that if you meditate while twisted to the left or the right, rather than facing forwards, you can bring on some weird sensations and experiences which are usually unhelpful or unpleasant.

Your jaw and tongue - the fourth point is your jaw and tongue. Your jaw should be relaxed, teeth slightly apart, with your tongue resting upon your upper palate, just behind the back of the teeth, to prevent excess salivation. Your lips can be slightly apart also.

Your head - the fifth point is your head. Tuck your chin in so that your neck extends and your head tilts ever so slightly forward. This helps to extend the spine naturally. If your head is held too high, you will find that mental wandering, agitation, and excitation accelerates and intensifies. If your head is tilted too far forward, you'll find this brings on more dullness and sleepiness.

Your eyes – your eyes can be either slightly open, with your gaze directed downwards naturally towards the floor in front of you, or they can be lightly closed, or they can just be naturally open. Again, that's something that you'll experiment with and also something that can change depending on the meditation that you practice. Meditating with your eyes naturally open is a beneficial skill to cultivate. It breaks the assumption that the mind is somewhere behind the eyes and helps us integrate our mindfulness practice into daily life, where our eyes are usually open.

Your shoulders – and the seventh point is your shoulders. Your shoulders should be level and relaxed. This also helps maintain the rest of your posture and helps to maintain stillness.

This posture has been taught and used for centuries by both very experienced, dedicated yogis and newbies alike, and for excellent reason. The point of this posture is to help our energy flow properly, and it is the most beneficial for sustained periods of meditation, concentration, and contemplation. It helps prevent the two sides of attentional imbalance – sleepiness and dullness, agitation, and distraction – as far as possible from a purely physical perspective. On a personal note, I have found it helpful too for another reason. As you ascertain your ideal posture and go through the points one by one, you begin the process of focusing your attention and bringing your awareness out of the mental domain and into the body. By figuring out the posture and putting everything in the right place, you're already pulling away from the rumination and focusing elsewhere. As best you can, if you're doing your meditation in a seated position, try to follow this posture, and you will notice the benefits.

If you decide to lie down for the meditation, do your best approximation of the *shavasana*, or corpse pose, taught in yoga. You can be completely relaxed as you fully surrender your muscles to gravity and let everything become loose and relaxed. To help keep you alert and prevent you from falling asleep, however, you want to adopt a *psychological* posture of vigilance. This means lying down and maintaining alertness as you would if you had a newborn baby in the next room, hot boiling water on the stove, or bread in the toaster. Although you're lying down, maintain vigilance so that you could get up at a moment's notice if you needed to; don't drift off and allow yourself to become sleepy. For the actual posture, you should be lying flat on your back with your feet slightly apart, your arms slightly away from your body, both about 30 degrees, with your palms facing upwards. You might want to place a small cushion behind the head if that improves your comfort. The room should be softly lit and keep a blanket handy if you need to. The supine position is perfect for emphasising relaxation, so please experiment with that from time to time.

Guided Meditation: Present-Centring 🎧

Find a comfortable posture in which you can be quite relaxed and still. If you are seated, use the seven-point meditation posture, and if you are lying down, then use the shavasana. Your eyes may be closed or partially open. Relax into this posture and take some time to settle, breathing into any areas that seem tense. Bring to mind your most meaningful aspiration for this practice so that it may be of benefit to yourself and others.

Begin the practice by bringing yourself into the present moment with five very significant and purposeful breaths. Fully inhale, expanding the belly and chest as much as you can, hold it for a moment, and exhale gently, feeling a wave of relaxation sweep over you. Do this five times, extending the exhale each time, and feel your body relax more and more. When we're stressed or anxious, we breathe in very unhealthy ways. Taking a moment to breathe deeply and fully is an expression of self-compassion.

Once you've finished those deep breaths, allow your breathing to return to normal and take note of how you feel at this very moment. Bring your awareness to the top of your head and notice how it feels. There's no need to think about the top of the head, but simply notice how it feels - any throbbing, tingling, vibration, or sense of temperature. Gradually, let your focus move down to your eyes, noticing sensations as your focus moves. Notice how your eyes feel and ask them to relax. Allow your eyes to soften. Move your awareness around to the back of the head, noticing how that feels. If the back of your head is resting against a surface, notice too how that contact feels. Notice how heavy your head feels right now. Allow your focus to move down to your nose, feeling the slight sensations of the air moving in and out with your breath. Bring awareness to your ears and notice how they feel. Notice sounds around you, and when a sound comes in, let it act as a little wave of relaxation, taking you even deeper into the present moment. As you bring your awareness down to your mouth, let sounds fade into the background once more. Notice how your mouth feels. Move your focus down your neck and shoulders. If you find any tension along the way, ask it to release, and especially on the outbreath, make that intention to release and relax more and more deeply. Slowly take your attention down each arm, all the way to each fingertip. Feel the sensations of touch at your fingertips. Bring awareness to your chest and your upper back, also relaxing these areas. If there is any tension, again, release it on the outbreath as you relax. Focus on your heart, feel it beating, supporting you, keeping you alive. Take a moment to feel gratitude for your heart. Experience the *sensations in your lungs as they gently expand and contract with your breath, bringing in oxygen to your body. Feel gratitude for your lungs. Move your awareness down gradually to your abdomen, noticing sensations as your attention moves. Feel your belly and all the sensations in and around the abdomen. Observe your lower back, and if it rests against any surface, and notice how that contact feels. If you feel any tension here as well, on the outbreath, release and relax. Focus on your pelvis and your hips, feeling any sensations here. As you move lower into the body, allow a deeper state of relaxation to manifest. Move your awareness down each leg, slowly relaxing them. Your legs do so much for you, so give them this gift of relaxation. Allow a delightful wave of relaxation to move down to your feet and the tips of your toes.*

Once you have completed your body scan, allow your awareness to fill the entire space of the body. To the best of your ability, without following any thoughts about the past or the future, rest right here, right now. Be present with the space of the body and the sensations within it.

You cannot experience your body in the past or the future. When you are present with and experiencing the body, you are in the present moment. Being present with your body allows you to be present in your life.

Before closing the meditation, dedicate the positive energy or merit that you've generated to your highest aspirations and intentions. Close with a few words of loving-kindness and compassion, such as "May all beings find happiness and the causes of happiness. May all beings be free of suffering and the causes of suffering."

1 - Cultivating Mindfulness Through a Regular Meditation Practice

Our first way of living more mindfully is through cultivating a regular meditation practice. Meditation need not be something mysterious, esoteric, or difficult to do. It is simply the process of directing our awareness to a chosen object and cultivating our mind. We often think of meditation in terms of the very formal practice, sitting on a cushion on the floor, eyes closed, shut off from the world. It can be interesting to go back to the roots and real meaning. The Pali word for meditation is *bhāvanā*, and literally means "development" or "cultivation". A farmer performs *bhāvanā* when they prepare the soil and plant their crops. We perform *citta-bhāvanā* (*citta* meaning mind) any time we cultivate or develop our mind. This activity is therefore not isolated to a meditation cushion.

I've heard people say that meditation is too difficult to do or is boring and unengaging. In this case,
the idea of what meditation is may have become too
complex or the practitioner may be pushing too hard.
We can look at it from another angle. Imagine you are
in your garden, or on a park bench. It's a sunny, fresh
day, and you are sitting quietly. It's not particularly exciting, but you're still getting pleasure from having
this quiet moment to relax, enjoying time away from
work and responsibilities, even though you are not
really stimulated or engaged in an activity. Now, imagine that instead of keeping your eyes open, you
close your eyes. You can still hear everything outside:
the sound of the wind, nature, people talking,
vehicles in the distance. You are aware they are out
there. Now and again, random thoughts come up;
some are funny, some are interesting, some create
fear, and some make you sad. Nevertheless, if you focus once again, you can become aware of the various
sounds around you again. Meditation can be just that.
In this example, your *object of meditation* is sound,
and you are practising mindfulness of sound. You allow yourself to be aware of whatever sounds come

up, and when you get lost in your own thoughts or thinking about a sound, instead of fighting it or resisting it, you simply leave it behind and come back to your object of meditation. There's nothing more to do other than to rest in the stillness and enjoy this precious moment of calm. You can do this simple meditation with other objects too, such as something you can see in front of you or a tactile sensation like the breath, as we will explore in this section. You can start by practising for just three minutes. If you feel three minutes is overwhelming, practice for only one minute. If, over time, you feel that three minutes is easy, then do five, then 10. Let your practice evolve and accommodate your current mental state and concentration skills.

Meditation is also how we train our concentration. This is called training our faculty of mindfulness. How do we train mindfulness in meditation? In the Buddhist tradition, we train mindfulness through *shamatha* meditation, and we apply our mindfulness through *vipassana* meditation.

Shamatha is often translated as *meditative quiescence* or *tranquil abiding* and refers to a state in which our mind is calm, stable, clear, and focused. Although this mind is very calm and relaxed, it is not dull. Often, we confuse being quite relaxed with taking a nap, or spacing out, or daydreaming, but the mind of shamatha is very poised, serviceable, and ready to be put to use. The method by which we achieve shamatha is essentially a process of training our ability to hold our attention on a single object, such as the breath, for longer and longer periods. As you may have experienced for yourself, when we engage in this training, we experience various challenges. The main challenge to balancing our attention are the two sides of attentional imbalance – *laxity*, which is the experience of dullness, spacing out, mental sinking, and becoming sleepy – and *excitation*, which is the experience of mental wandering, distraction, and agitation. Nowadays, attention deficit and hyperactivity are the norms, even outside of meditation. Most of the time, our attention either constantly flits from one thing to another (remember the monkey mind), and we're unable to bring it under control, or our attention is so lax that we cannot concentrate for more than a few minutes before we become unfocused, bored, and sleepy. Because of this inability to control where our attention goes, we experience a lot of difficulties on a daily basis. Work or study can be challenging, negative thoughts seem incessant and unstoppable, and even building and maintaining relationships can be difficult. Anyone who has ever tried meditation will be familiar with how out of control the mind can be, jumping from one thought to the next. I've heard people say that they feel like meditation makes their mind busier, but in reality, what's happening is that we're becoming aware of how busy and turbulent the mind always was. Training in shamatha is all about taking ourselves gradually from our starting point of only being able to hold our attention on the breath for a few seconds, to being able to do it unwaveringly for hours on end. It is called meditation *practice* for a reason, so be patient with yourself in the beginning.

The achievement of shamatha itself is an incredible achievement and one that most will not achieve or even aspire to unless you consider yourself a Buddhist aspiring to achieve enlightenment for the sake of all living beings. The achievement of shamatha requires rigorous training for potentially months on end in a secluded retreat environment. So, why engage in shamatha training or even talk about it at all? In parallel, most of us will also not become Olympic-level athletes. However, we can still benefit from the practices, insights, and discoveries made by highly achieved athletes if we wish to improve our physical health and wellbeing through diet and exercise. Likewise, there is much to be gained by training our attention through meditation, and exploring the insights and discoveries made by those who have achieved shamatha in the past. This can be very beneficial in helping us succeed in meditation.

So, what makes a shamatha meditation a shamatha meditation? Any meditation – whether Buddhist in origin or not – where the aim is to focus your attention single-pointedly on one particular object, such as the breath, a mental image, or even a pebble, or a stick, is a shamatha meditation. This is because any meditation where you focus single-pointedly on one thing will cultivate and train your faculty of mindfulness and attention skills.

Why Meditate?

Training our attention doesn't just improve the quality of our meditations. Any activity in life which requires us to focus our attention well can be improved. As B. Alan Wallace says in his book *The Attention Revolution:*

> *"Few things affect our lives more than our faculty of attention. If we can't focus our attention – due to either agitation or dullness – we can't do anything well. We can't study, listen, converse with others, work, play, or even sleep well when our attention is impaired. And for many of us, our attention is impaired much of the time...*
>
> *Our faculty of attention affects us in countless ways. Our very perception of reality is tied closely to where we focus our attention. Only*

> *what we pay attention to seems real to us,
> whereas whatever we ignore - no matter how
> important it may be - seems to fade into in-
> significance."*

As we cultivate the ability to place our attention where it needs to be voluntarily, we find that we carry less agitation and stress. With better mental balance, comes less craving, and less attachment. We start to become masters of our mind instead of being the slaves of our mind. We start to enjoy simple pleasures in life more, without clinging to them and being afraid of losing them. Our quality of sleep improves, and we experience physical health benefits too. Clearly, we can see the benefit that a focused mind can bring to our lives and the disadvantages of a mind that is constantly caught up in one distraction after another.

Many people report that meditation is a great way to start or end their day. Daily practice has ripple effects almost immediately in our life. People who come along to our meditation classes regularly share with me that when they start up a regular meditation practice, they experience benefits in their way of being and interacting with the world and other people almost immediately. Some, in only the second week of an introductory course, shared that they were already discovering that with regular practice, they were able to be more patient, more balanced, and calmer when things went wrong in their day. They found that they had a bit more mental space, and they'd started to get a sense of an ability to pause, breathe, and choose a different reaction to difficulties. Just by introducing a short period in the day where the mind can be quiet and balanced, the healing and soothing qualities of that experience were carried throughout the rest of the day. This is no surprise because, in meditation, we immerse the mind in an experience which is entirely the opposite to the rest of our day, where we are distracted by a million thoughts an hour. Even five to 10 minutes a day can be beneficial and very healing at the beginning. By engaging in a regular practice, we'll start introducing this quality of slowing down, being calm, and being present with our daily experience.

Everyone Can Meditate

With all these benefits to be experienced, if we haven't got a regular meditation practice yet, it begs the question, why? One reason which many people tell me is, "I can't meditate! I tried, but I just got distracted over and over. It was exhausting." I am very firm in my belief that everyone can meditate. If you've been able to hold your attention on the breath even very briefly for a second or two before you became distracted entirely for the rest of your meditation, then you've already achieved stage one of the classic presentation of the nine stages to shamatha. The bar is low because we all start from the same place. So, even if every time you meditate it's not long before you get very distracted or fall asleep, and all you discover is that your mind is very turbulent and noisy, this is progress.

Most people go through their entire life without any idea how busy their mind is. Without that discovery, they never come to understand the parallel between their turbulent mental state and their unsatisfying physical reality, nor do they feel motivated to do anything about it.

I affirm that you can meditate, but like anything we want to get good at, it's a skill. You wouldn't expect to pick up a guitar and be playing at Wembley Stadium after your first try, so we shouldn't expect to be able to maintain our attention on the breath perfectly for 10 whole minutes when we first start. The entire point of the theoretical framework of the nine stages of shamatha and the wealth of material behind it is to help us go from this point of being a complete beginner to gradually becoming one who reaps the benefits of meditation.

There is an antidote or a tool for all the challenging experiences we experience on our meditation path. As we progress, we learn to delicately maintain a balance between the two extremes of attentional imbalance, like a bird maintaining a perfect balance in the wind by just slightly moving its wings.

As you practice the meditations and explore the tools shared in this book and seek guidance for any hindrances you're experiencing from a qualified teacher, your meditation will go from being 10 minutes of just being completely distracted – or 10 minutes of sleep – to a very enjoyable, soothing experience. The key is to give yourself the time to practice and the patience to work through the challenges along the way. I encourage you to experiment with meditating both sitting down and lying down to find what works best for you to find that relaxing, enjoyable, soothing experience that then has a ripple effect in your life.

One of the crucial things to note here is about expectations. When we first start up a mediation practice, we want it to give us some immediate, amazing effects, and if it doesn't, then we lose all motivation to do more. It is best to practice without grasping onto our desire for something (or nothing) to happen. As best you can, practice without expectations. What happens is exactly what is meant to happen at this stage. The next important piece of advice is to prioritise quality over quantity. It is far better to meditate well for five minutes several times a day than to proclaim that we meditate for two hours every day, but we're entirely distracted for one hour and 50 minutes of that period. The time is not important; the quality is. If we meditate for long periods but are either distracted or asleep, we may cultivate a bad habit that will become difficult to overcome later on. Rest assured, as our practice starts to improve and we experience the peace and wellbeing that arises from it, our motivation and enthusiasm to practice will naturally increase. Effort is needed initially as we train our mindfulness, but the level of effort required reduces over time once we break through those initial issues of mental wandering and sleepiness. Once you're past that break and you've found yourself on the other side, meditation is a gratifying experience.

Why Mindfulness of Breathing?

"Just as in the last month of the hot season, when a mass of dust and dirt has swirled up, a great rain cloud out of season disperses it and quells it on the spot, so too concentration by mindfulness of breathing, when developed and cultivated, is peaceful, sublime, an ambrosial dwelling, and it disperses and

quells on the spot unwholesome states whenever they arise." - The Buddha (Saṃyutta Nikāya 54.9)

The Buddha describes the experience of concentration by way of mindfulness of breathing as "peaceful", "sublime" ,"an ambrosial dwelling", and that it "disperses and quells on the spot unwholesome states whenever they arise".

So, that first experience is of peace and calm, and we've all probably experienced that if we've done some meditation. The simple experience of giving the body and mind a break from the distractions and noise is very peaceful and very calming. As we go deeper in practice, a sense of feeling really well and healthy in the body and mind arises. And then, it is followed by something quite interesting and entirely unexpected: an experience of bliss or joy. You wouldn't think that attending to something like the breath would be very interesting, and you wouldn't consider that it would give rise to an experience of bliss or joy. Still, this report has been corroborated repeatedly by practitioners over thousands of years and isn't something that we need to be very advanced in our practice to experience for ourselves.

So, by practising mindfulness of breathing, we experience peace and calm, then a feeling of well-being arises, followed by a sense of bliss or joy, and then following these states comes a mind which – as the Buddha described – "dispels and quells unwholesome states whenever they arise." And this means that thoughts of worry, stress, or anger might try to arise in the mind, but, like a fish swimming against a powerful current, as they try to do so, they struggle against the strong current of the mind and cannot get a footing.

So, as we gain familiarity with this kind of experience on a daily basis, and we're connecting more and more with this peaceful, clear, luminous state of mind – which is its true nature below the neuroses and noise of daily life – the days get easier. We will start to experience less frustration, less disappointment related to the outside world, and less boredom. We feel less inclined to want to distract ourselves so much and fill our mind with nonsense because we're in touch with such an amazing quality of mind that we didn't have access to before.

This then has a knock-on effect by helping us live mindfully, too, so not only do we get the benefits from the meditation practice itself, but it supports us with the other practices explored in this book. I would say that regular meditation practice is an essential foundation that we need to utilise mindfulness in the other four areas we are going to explore. If we have some regular practice and experience of mindfulness of breathing, then there are two main ways this will help us later on. The first is that it counteracts this chronic distractibility and the noise and turbulence that plagues our mind. As a result of this, we'll find it easier to introduce awareness into our day and culti-vate awareness of what's going on in our mind. The second benefit is that we're actively training our mindfulness. Remember that mindfulness means "to remember without forgetting" and is literally the abili-ty to "bear in mind". In meditation, we are training ourselves to "bear in mind" the breath. So, we're train-ing our concentration, our ability to focus, and our ability to remember. That will translate into other areas of our life, and we'll find the other mindful practices introduced in this book easier because of that.

Guided Meditation: Mindfulness of Breathing 🎧

Find a comfortable posture in which you can be quite relaxed and still. If you are seated, use the seven-point meditation posture, and if you are lying down, then use the shavasana. Your eyes may be closed or partially open. Relax into this posture and take some time to settle. Bring to mind your most meaningful aspiration for this practice so that it may be of benefit to yourself and others.

Begin the practice by first settling your body, speech, and mind in their natural states. First, ground your awareness by allowing it to descend from the head into the body, right down to the ground where you are in contact with the cushion, the chair, or the floor. This space is non-conceptual, so likewise, let your awareness rest in a witnessing mode – not thinking about the body or adding any thoughts about what you find, but simply attending to the raw, tactile sensations you experience. Let your awareness fill the entire space of the body and spend a few moments resting with the felt sensations of the body, again in a witnessing mode. As you rest in the body, you may notice areas of tension or tightness, as you do, breathe into those areas and invite yourself to relax and release that tension with the outbreath. Bring your attention to your face, and make sure the muscles of the forehead, eyes, cheeks, jaws, and mouth are relaxed. Settle your body in its natural state imbued with these three qualities: relaxation, stillness, and vigilance.

Ensure that your posture is not restricting the breathing in any way and allow the belly to be soft. While letting your respiration be completely natural, let every outbreath be a new opportunity to relax more and more in the body, releasing any tension, relaxing the muscles, and also releasing any thoughts that may be trying to captivate your attention.

Allow yourself the freedom to set aside any hopes or concerns about the past or the future, and even any thoughts about the present and about how the medi-

tation is or isn't progressing. Release all expectations and all grasping, and let your awareness come to rest in the present moment, fully aware of the body.

Out of the stillness of body and awareness, begin to notice the rhythmic sensations in the body that are correlated with the in and the outbreath. Notice the gentle ebb and flow, the rise and fall, the vibration and tingling, all the movements of energy throughout the body as you breathe in and breathe out. You may notice sensations in the belly, the chest, the sensation of air at the nostrils. You may even detect fluctuations of movement in the arms, legs, and head. The whole body is breathing, so be aware of the whole body breathing.

As the meditation progresses, allow yourself to relax more and more deeply with every outbreath. Relaxation and stillness are of paramount importance. Relaxation and stillness; stillness observing motion.

You may notice from time to time that your mind wanders, and you have been captivated by thoughts. This is natural and to be expected. We counteract this agitation with relaxation. When you notice distraction, don't tense up, don't tighten, don't constrict. Instead, let your first reaction be to relax, then release the thought with the outbreath, and return your attention.

If, on the other hand, you notice that you are becoming a bit dull, a bit vague, spaced out, or sleepy, then refresh your interest. Refresh your motivation for the practice and focus more closely on the breath. You may also find it useful to open your eyes ever so slightly to let some light in. Ensure that as the meditation progresses your head does not tilt forward or to the side but remains balanced.

Before closing the meditation, dedicate the positive energy or merit that you've generated to your highest aspirations and intentions. Close with a few words of loving-kindness and compassion, such as "May all beings find happiness and the causes of happiness. May all beings be free of suffering and the causes of suffering".

I encourage you to practice once a day for one week with the above meditation and experiment with different postures if you wish. It is OK to do very short meditations; you do not need to rush for 20 minutes at first if this is difficult.

When we first practice meditation, we may notice that we are particularly prone to distraction or that our mind does become dull. It's important here that we are kind to ourselves and remember that we have a type of addiction. We're addicted to chronic distractibility and mental wandering, and in our waking life, there is constant stimulus going on. In meditation, we are going against the grain, and we're going against the addiction that we have. We should recognise that laxity and excitation are the norm and are withdrawal symptoms. The mind is going from being very active and on the go to being quite still and focusing on one thing. I often say that it is like giving a kid lots of sugary sweets and ice cream, telling them you're going to take them to Disneyland, and then asking them to sit quietly. It takes time to overcome addiction and a lifetime of mental training. We should recognise that it is inevitable that we will experience these hindrances, especially as we start up a meditation practice. Still, we should be kind to ourselves and remember that it does take time and that it is a skill we're training. Even if you were quite distracted, you might notice that you feel more peaceful and calmer than you did before your meditation. That on its own is a win and something worth making a note of.

Questions and Responses

Question: Mental wandering is a common problem for me. But also, something I picked up on in my meditation, when you said "don't control your breath" I immediately controlled it. So, by saying not to control it, it then made me control it more?

Response: Before I tell you not to control it, are you just letting it be natural anyway? Because if so, then ignore my instruction. Ignore me when I ask you to leave it natural if it's natural already. The reason I say it is because a lot of people don't realise, but they are either sitting in a certain way that's constricting the breath or, the breath is very responsive to our mind, so when we get anxious, if we get anxious thoughts, our breath starts to change immediately. So many people are not aware that they are controlling their breath, especially when they're focused on it. So, for many, the more intensely they focus, the more they control their breathing. So, if you're confident that it is natural anyway, then ignore my instruction as best you can, but take a closer look and see, as you attend to the breath, are you controlling it even subtly? If so, that's something you need to work on. We need to rest our awareness on the sensations of the breath passively. In terms of my instruction, if you get stuck there, go back to the felt sensations once more. The sensations are non-conceptual, they don't have any labels, they don't tell you "you're controlling me" or not. So, if you're stuck there, try to release that thought, "am I controlling it or not?" and go back to bare attention, simply witnessing as best you can. I heard you also say that the main barrier you'd found to a regular practice was mental wandering, right? That is a very common one.

Question: That's right, yeah. That's the main one, really. The monkey mind, jumping from branch to branch, that's my experience. I always want to get somewhere, but then I follow a thought about something I want; there's always the next thing, the next thing, the next thing.

Response: Yeah, I think you hit the nail on the head – it's the monkey mind jumping from branch to branch. There's always something better, there's always something bigger, always something new, always something else to look forward to. That is mostly this mind of attachment that we have, and again it's about that addiction, isn't it? In meditation in particular, if we find mental wandering a problem, the antidote for that is actually relaxation. It is to relax more, and that's what we need to emphasise more in our practice. When we get distracted, we get tense and want to force our attention, but this only gives the agitation more energy. The antidote really is to relax, loosen up more.

Question: With the mind wandering, because I struggle with that as well, the more you meditate, does that become easier?

Response: Yes, it does. There are these nine stages of shamatha that I mentioned. The whole point of our practice of mindfulness of breathing is that we're trying to balance these two – whichever one we have more of – the sleepiness or the excitation - we're trying to balance that over time. So, we use different tools that will work for us, for example, counting the breaths, until our mindfulness gets stronger and our introspection more effective. It's about cultivating strong mindfulness, and what we're doing in these meditations is we're training our mindfulness. So, the stronger our mindfulness becomes, the less these wandering thoughts can get in. And then, when we get our mind to such a point that it is relaxed, we don't have to make an effort to remember the breath anymore because it happens through familiarisation. On the stages of this shamatha path, we see that a lot of effort is required initially, and in the end, it's all about familiarisation because the mind knows what it needs to do. But yeah, it definitely gets easier, and they stop being so incessant. The flow of thoughts are likened to a really fast waterfall, to begin with, and then, in the end, it's an ocean unmoved by waves, is the description in the literature. So yes, it does get easier.

Question: I've still got to find the right and most appropriate time for me. I don't seem to have found that yet. But actually, I know what it is. I think I've got to sit down, just really prioritise getting the appropriate time, rather than just suddenly think, "Oh, I'll do my meditation now", you know, which is probably what sort of happens. That day I'll think, "Oh, I'll do it in the morning" or "I don't feel like doing it in the morning, I want to have a shower, I'll do it later". I think for me, I do need to find the right time and to keep in the structure; otherwise, I'll forget to do it.

Response: Yeah, definitely. I think a big part of our training is all about finding the right combination of all these things; the right meditation, you know, which area of the breath is good for us, which posture is good for us, what time of day is good for us, and build that habit. There's a combination there that works for you, and you've just got to find it, and perhaps it is a certain time of day, or perhaps it's just before a shower or perhaps it's after a shower – there's no way of telling what it is, except for experimenting, isn't it? And I know what you mean about wanting to meditate when you feel inspired to, and usually, those are some of the best meditations we have!

Question: Once we're getting the benefits from meditation, will we want to do it more?

Response: Absolutely! Once you have those good meditations, once it starts to really work for you and you start to experience that peace, as I said, the enthusiasm naturally comes to want to meditate more. I remember in the first retreat I did, I spent quite a few hours doing just mindfulness of breathing, and at first, the mind struggled, but the more I did it, the more I actually wanted to do. The enthusiasm for the practice really does come from just doing it. If I had the option to watch TV or listen to some music or do some more meditation, I'd surprise myself, and I would think, "Hmm, actually, I want to meditate because I know I'll enjoy that more". So, the enthusiasm comes from the practice, so it's not all, sort of, hard graft all the way, it's just at the start, until we start to enjoy it and it starts to work for us.

2 – Leading a Meaningful and Deliberate Life

From the moment we wake up until the moment we go to sleep, many of us are on autopilot, responding to the five physical senses: what we can see, what we can hear, whatever is coming up in our immediate environment but without being very mentally aware of it. Our thoughts and emotions are a little bit all over the place, overly thinking about the past, worrying about the future. As we go through our days and our weeks it can feel like we're not very present. It's as if we're here in the body going about our day, and as my Dad used to say, "the lights are on but nobody's home"! So while the body is going about its day, our mind is elsewhere. The mind is worrying, it's remembering, there's turbulence, distraction and it's not really present with the body. There is a disconnect between, specifically, our awareness, mind, and body. By awareness I'm referring to that part of the mind that we would say is the agent or the sovereign. For example, if I told you to look to your left and look at something that's next to you and observe its colour, how it looks, it's that part of your mind that becomes aware of and attends to that object. Or, if I said "pink elephant" and you imagine the pink elephant in your mind, your awareness is that part of your mind that attends to these objects. There's a disconnect here between our awareness, our mind, our body, and what's going on in our mind and our body.

Our awareness is like a balloon that we're holding onto, and our thoughts and emotions are like the wind, and we're holding this balloon in the midst of a storm on the beach, and it is being blown all over the place by thoughts, memories, and emotions that we don't seem to have any control of. The downside of this is that we're living in a way that means we experience more mental pain, more anxiety, more stress, more frustration than we actually need to because we don't have control over our experience. We don't have control over that balloon, and we're left at the mercy of our external world and our uncontrolled thoughts.

Mindful living is about coming in out of that storm to a calm place where there is no strong breeze, where our awareness can be relatively still and be present with whatever's happening in the body and the mind.

The second way for us to introduce mindfulness into our daily life is by leading a meaningful and deliberate life, and that's about being mindful of the choices that we make in our day-to-day life, and mindful of our faculty of conation:

> *"Those desiring to escape from suffering, hasten right towards their own misery. And with the very desire for happiness, out of delusion, they destroy their own wellbeing as if it were the enemy."* – *Shantideva*

Buddhist psychology highlights that every sentient being, from the tiniest of creatures to the largest, has two instinctual desires: to be happy, and to be free of suffering. This is true for us, and it isn't difficult to see how it influences our every decision and our every action. But despite this instinctual desire to be happy, well, comfortable, and fulfilled, and despite all our actions and decisions being driven by this, we still seem to experience mental suffering, frustration, and anxiety. We have periods of being happy, but there seems to be an underlying dissatisfaction or discontentment in our life.

So, what is Shantideva talking about here in this quote? For this, we look at this term "conation", which is a term known really well in psychology but it's not a part of our common vocabulary. Conation is our mental faculty of purpose, desire, or volition. It's the part of our mind that is responsible for what our purpose is and what our desires are. Seeing the importance of conation in our wellbeing, Lama Alan has coined this term *conative intelligence*. He describes it as our ability to determine which desires and intentions truly lead to our own and others' wellbeing, and the ability to adopt those ones while releasing those desires and intentions that undermine our own and others' wellbeing.

Humans have access to a truly incredible level of intelligence. It might not seem like it sometimes, but when we look at what was evolutionarily required for humans to survive and procreate, we've developed a level far above what was necessary, compared to other species. We are able to share our learnings and understandings through language, from generation to generation. With this advanced intelligence and ability to teach and learn, you'd think that generation on generation, we'd become happier humans. Combine our desire for happiness with this intelligence, then, on an individual level and on a global level, we should be getting closer. When we're younger - in our teens especially - we're very unsettled, we haven't figured things out yet. We've stuck our hand in a candle and found out that it burns and learnt some lessons, but we're still learning and we're still taking everything very seriously. As we get older, we become wiser, and some people become calmer, and more *c'est la vie*. But others, not so much. Given our extraordinary levels of intelligence, memory, and imagination, the question comes up - why are we as a species and as individuals, not becoming happier with every generation and with each year of our lives? This comes down to our pursuit of happiness, our understanding of what happiness really is, where we seek it, and the choices that we make then in that pursuit. His Holiness the Dalai Lama is often quoted as saying: "I believe that the very purpose of our life is to seek happiness. Whether we believe in religion or not, or this religion, or that religion, we're all seeking something better in life, so the very motion of our life is toward happiness." I think we could all agree with that statement. If we weren't looking for something better, more lasting, would we be reading this book?

What is the disconnect here between this desire to have something better, the choices we make, and the life we end up with? There seems to be a bit of a disconnect between these three. I believe it comes down to the fact that, under the influence of our mental afflictions, we make unwise choices that later lead to our own frustration, disappointment, misery, or stress, because we mix up the two types of happiness too often.

The Two Types of Happiness

As explored previously, there are two types of happiness and wellbeing that have been discovered by contemplatives for generations. The first type is *hedonia*, or hedonic pleasure, to use the Greek term, which is pleasure and happiness derived from the external world. This pleasure is dependent upon having good circumstances or having stimulation. The second type is *eudaemonia*, another Greek term that we could call genuine or authentic happiness. This second domain of happiness comes from within: it is our own inner genuine wellbeing, and it's about what we bring to the world not what we get from it. It is therefore not dependent upon having good circumstances or having stimulation.

We believe that happiness comes from having a good meal, or from having the best, latest new phone, the flashy car outside, or money, fame, reputation. We believe that a happy, fulfilled life will come out of having these things, but our experience tells us that it doesn't. Authentic and lasting happiness comes from within.

There are many arguments for demonstrating this fact. For example, we see those people in society who have the most: the most money, fame, reputation, are some of the most unhappy people. Everybody is familiar with celebrity dramas and addictions being displayed all over magazines, newspapers, and social media, so this is common. If fame or money brought happiness, then would these people not be glaring examples of the happiest, most fulfilled, and content people around?

On the other side, we see some of the poorest in our society or those who are going through challenges with physical illness, as some of the happiest, most content people in our society. If having more was the cause of happiness, then we'd see that those people were happier and we'd be able to measure happiness levels by measures of fame or money.

In addition, what makes something a cause of happiness or suffering is internal, not external. If external things from their own side were causes of happiness or suffering from their own side, then we'd also see that everyone would have the same response. Everybody would enjoy golf, but many people don't enjoy golf. Everybody would get stressed at deadlines, but some people don't get stressed at deadlines. External things are not causes of happiness or suffering from their own side.

Our way of mistaking things also means we are disempowering ourselves. We perceive material possession and external events as causes of happiness and pleasure from their own side, almost as if our mind plays no role. For example, some say that walking on the beach makes them happy. In reality, whatever pleasurable or joyful feeling we get from the external world comes from the side of the mind. We can see from our own experience that when we are upset or angry, our possessions can mean nothing to us; we may throw them against a wall or break them. When our mind is disturbed, our collection of good things isn't able to protect us and provide us with the comfort we seek. If we are upset, angry, or stressed, then our walk on the beach becomes full of faults – it's too windy, too hot, too cold, too wet, too noisy, and so on. If the walk on the beach truly was a cause of happiness from its own side, and our mind had no role to play, then everyone would enjoy this experience and immediately become happy, no matter how they felt previously or what mind they brought with them. We know this to not be true. If we have a sour mind, even the most enjoyable experiences can be ruined, and not everyone enjoys a walk on the beach!

The important point is that after you have enough – enough to not have to worry, enough to not have to stress about your next meal – you don't get any happier as you acquire more. If you have twice as much money as you need, you don't get to become twice as happy, or five times as happy, or 10 times as happy. Once these things have brought you to a point, and you have an education, a roof over your head, you have these comforts and your basics, and the stress or worry associated with not having them has subsided – you don't get any happier from having more. You will still experience frustration, anxiety, stress, and many would argue you will experience more of this the more you acquire.

What is the point of exploring this point again? Well, our way of living and our way of pursuing happiness externally shows that we don't understand this point. We still believe we need more. Our lives are characterised by thoughts of "as soon as I get this, as soon as I get that", or "I just need this". This way of craving and chasing after new possessions and experiences, getting frustrated at what we can't have, and disappointed by what we do have, is the reason behind so much of our day-to-day suffering.

We Sometimes Make Unwise Choices

From the point of view of our own wellbeing and happiness, we sometimes make unwise choices. We make choices that lead to our own frustration and our own stress later on because we're mixing up the two types of happiness.

As an example, perhaps instead of finishing an important task at work or completing an essay for university, we decide we're going to watch a whole series on Netflix or go out with friends instead. It might feel great at the time but then later on lead to some deadline anxiety or a feeling of stress and overwhelm. We were looking for pleasure, or moving away from overwhelm, and in the end found the opposite. When on a diet, perhaps we go for a quick win and eat a whole tub of ice cream and down a bottle of wine. This is another one that might feel great at first, but then we suffer for later on, making ourselves feel bad by being overly self-critical, judging ourselves, and feeding into our low self-esteem. Some get lost in the moment and drink a little too much, only to suffer the next day. We've all seen or known someone who drank too much, ended up in an argument with family or friends that perhaps remains unresolved, or even escalated to a fight in the street. All of these choices, some more obviously unwise than the others, came down to our desire to experience pleasure, happiness, or joy, and making a choice which then, instead of bringing us the lasting happiness that we were initially looking for, brought us or others harm. Instead of filling the hole we were feeling, it left us with more regret later on. It's important to recognise what I'm saying here. A Netflix series, going out with friends, or ice-cream is not the problem. Enjoying these things is not unwise. However, looking to these things as sources of lasting pleasure or as solutions to unhappiness is unwise.

To understand this disconnect and to be able to introduce mindfulness to our choices – to live a purposeful and meaningful life – we need to be really clear on what constitutes genuine mental wellbeing for us, what we could call "the types of happiness that I want to experience". With an understanding of this, we then look at the types of unhappiness that we currently experience, and look back to the choices we made that lead to that unhappiness, understand what it means to have this conative intelligence and be mindful of our choices.

Three Domains of Wellbeing

Through direct first-person experience, many people from all walks of life, traditions, and disciplines, have empirically discovered that genuine happiness can be found through three specific domains: living an ethical way of life, cultivating exceptional mental balance, and generating wisdom.

In the *Kandaraka Sutta*, Majjhima Nikāya (I-346), we see that the Buddha himself described three types of genuine wellbeing that correlate with these discoveries. They are:

1. Wellbeing arising from a clear conscience and contentment.
2. Wellbeing gained through *samādhi*.
3. Supreme wellbeing of complete freedom through insight.

Wellbeing arising from a clear conscience and contentment

The first type is wellbeing arising from a clear conscience and contentment, or ethics. This refers to the wellbeing that comes from living an ethical way of life, from knowing that we are not causing harm in the world and that we are living a life of benevolence and non-violence. It's not difficult to see that if we're confident that our influence in the world is good and that we are not harming anyone, and we have done nothing wrong, that mental peace arises from this knowledge. If we feel we have done something wrong, if we often regret our actions and the way we behave through anger or stress, this leads to feeling like we're a bad person, guilt, or shame. This inhibits our ability to be happy. I was talking about this type of wellbeing during one of our retreats in Spain, and someone told me that that very morning while out on a walk, their neighbour's dog had escaped the garden and started a fight with her dog. Following the initial fear, and with adrenaline in her system, she became very angry with her neighbour and shouted at her. She made a comment which now, some hours later, she regretted, and which made her feel quite embarrassed and uneasy. The thought of having to now avoid this neighbour every time she came in and out of her house, whether the news would spread amongst the community, having this uncomfortable relationship with her neighbours, and being perceived as a bad person, left her with an unhappy feeling in the mind. This worry was disturbing her peace of mind, and she recognised that every time she would be reminded of this encounter these uneasy feelings would return. She decided then to leave her neighbour a note to apologise and to reconcile and repair the relationship that same day. I believe she did just that, and this feeling of unease and worry was lifted. Now, there was no need to relive the encounter and all the associated feelings, or avoid the neighbour, or move home altogether!

Wellbeing gained through samādhi

The second type of wellbeing coming from mental balance is about having access to that sense of wellbeing from within. This wellbeing is not contingent on having perfect external conditions and is instead found by cultivating a mind that is naturally serene, joyful, and content, rather than one that is just excited or aroused. This refers to the type of mind we achieve by training in shamatha, as described in the previous chapters. Most of us have experienced the enjoyment and peace that comes from being very concentrated and focused on something interesting - a hobby or skill, whether it be music, art, or science. There are some activities that we can enjoy being engaged in for hours on end and not have a problem being present, interested, and unwaveringly engaged. It is quite enjoyable and comforting to be fully engaged in this way. We've also experienced what it is like to bored to death by something - every minute moves slowly and we wish it would end. It's important to recognise what makes things boring is not objective. What makes things boring is the mind. If you bring a dull mind to anything, then what you attend to will be boring. Whether it is a film, a meal, a book, or time with family – anything can be boring – if you bring a dull quality of awareness to it. If, however, you have a concentrated, calm mind, anything is interesting, even watching your breath. With this quality of mind, boredom is gone. By training in meditation, we learn to cultivate this quality of awareness and then bring it to all our daily activities and interactions with others. This makes every part of our day interesting and engaging. It is also a very relaxing state of mind. The calmer our mind is, the greater the stability, the more composed it is, the greater stillness it has. The very quality of that awareness is deeply relaxing, contrary to our ordinary agitated mind.

Supreme wellbeing of complete freedom through insight

The third domain of wellbeing is through wisdom, and this is a truth-given joy. It's about knowing – not intellectually – but truly knowing from our own experience the nature of self, the world around us, and how things like our thoughts and emotions work. When we have more questions than answers and don't know why we experience mental suffering, how to get control of our mind, what the purpose of life is, or what we're even doing with our life, then our day-to-day experience can be very confusing and unsettling. We may wander through life, never having any awareness of the inner workings of the mind, blown around by our external world like a balloon in the wind, and get to the end of our life unsure of what it was all for. This truth-given joy is the opposite of a mid-life crisis: an utter confidence in what we're doing and why coming from our own understanding of how things really work and the nature of reality. There is a joy and an inner wellbeing that comes from having no uncertainty and no anxieties.

So, these are the three domains where there is genuine wellbeing, happiness, and flourishing to be found. With our lives imbued with these three qualities, it's not difficult to see how it would bring a deeper sense of happiness and joy to our life, no matter the circumstances we find ourselves in. We feel joy going about our day, with a warm-hearted and kind presence towards others, avoiding harm, content with what we have; we're experiencing a calm, steady state of mind, not an agitated one overloaded by stimulus; and we have an understanding that makes no experience confusing or without an answer – if a difficult emotion or challenging situation comes up, we have tools for dealing with them and are able to transform them quickly. It is not surprising then that training in these three areas became a central part of the Buddhist path. The *three higher trainings*, also called *the threefold training*, taught by the Buddha are:

1. The training in ethics (*sìla*) – also referred to as "higher virtue".
2. The training in concentration (*samādhi*) – also referred to as "higher mind".
3. The training in wisdom (*prajñā*) – also referred to as "higher wisdom".

These three practices, which are foundational to all Buddhist paths, can be taken as advice for a daily practice, as they encompass within them the entire

Noble Eightfold Path and the practices of the Six Perfections.[1]

The Two Types of Unhappiness

There are many ways to categorise and label the types of unhappiness we experience. To simplify, you could place them in two broad categories: stimulus-dependent and stimulus-independent.

The first is the type of unhappiness that is triggered by unpleasant circumstances, for example, by experiencing what we do not want to experience. It can feel that this is the type of unhappiness that the world imposes on us, but, upon further investigation, we find that while the unhappiness we experienced was *triggered* by stimulus, it did not arise from stimu-

---

1   The training of ethics includes Right Speech, Right Action, Right Livelihood, (The Noble Eightfold Path) and Generosity, Ethics, Patience (the Six Perfections). The training of concentration includes Right Effort, Right Mindfulness, Right Concentration, (The Noble Eightfold Path) and Concentration (the Six Perfections.) The training of wisdom includes Right View, Right Intention (The Noble Eightfold Path) and Wisdom (the Six Perfections).

lus alone, and the primary cause of the suffering was the subsequent reaction that happened in the mind.

The second type is the unhappiness that arises solely from within. This one can feel like it doesn't really have a trigger. We've all probably experienced these kinds of days where you just feel down, low energy, or tearful, and you don't really know why. Sometimes this can be a sign of physical ill-health; other times this is coming from stirrings in the mind that we do not yet have a sufficient level of self-awareness to detect.

Virtually any external or internal circumstance could trigger unhappiness for someone. The point that the Buddha so compassionately wants to wake us up to, however, is that the true causes of unhappiness are actually the imbalances and the afflictions of our mind, which at their source are the three root poisons of attachment, aversion, and ignorance. These three root afflictions are driving our addictions: addiction to sensory stimulation, obsessive compulsive ideation, not being able to sit still and not being able to sit quietly.

The Three Poisons

Attachment, or craving, is the first of the three. I like to refer to this one as "shiny toy syndrome". Attachment observes things outside of us that seem pleasurable, and falsely superimposes all of these amazing and desirable qualities upon it. It tells us how wonderful this new thing will be. It tells us "you really want this new phone, it's going to change your life". "You really want this new job, this new house, this new thing". It filters out and hides all its disagreeable qualities and anything that's bad about it, exaggerating its supposed desirable qualities. Then, under its influence, we see that thing as a source of pleasure and a source of happiness from its own side, and we must have it. This can be things like wealth, power, fame, or just stuff. Because of our way of viewing these things with attachment, we experience craving, which leads to unhappiness until we get it, jealousy of those who have it, frustration if we can't get it, and disappointment when we do get it and it bores us or the mind moves on. Attachment is also present in our relationships, the way we put conditions and expectations on other people and our world. We expect people to behave in a particular way, and then get upset when they don't. We then blame that unhappy feeling on them, when the actual cause was our own expectation. We're also very attached to our opinions, beliefs, and ways of seeing things. So much of the conflict in our world arises because of differing beliefs, and our inability to let go of these. Attachment leads to us being at odds with the world, which leads to mental unhappiness. We might take a moment to recognise how attachment or craving has afflicted us in the past or how it may be affecting our lives today.

Aversion or hostility, on the other hand, sees things as a source of unhappiness or a cause of our suffering from their own side. Just like with attachment, it distorts our perception of reality, and exaggerates any supposed negative qualities of an object, person or situation. We absolutely must avoid or harm such a thing that would bring about our suffering. This means we fear things going wrong, and we don't want to lose anything we like, so we cling on more tightly; we're angry at people and things that seem to be disagreeable, and we reject what we perceive be a threat.

Ignorance, the third poison, is how we misapprehend reality. The ways in which we misunderstand reality are numerous, but the Buddha taught that our unhappiness comes from the way we hold onto the impermanent as being permanent; things which are by nature unsatisfying as being sources of lasting satisfaction, and the not-self as being self.

The more our mind is dominated by these afflictions of attachment, aversion, and ignorance, and the more we act as a result of these delusions, the less free we'll be and the less genuine happiness we'll experience. We see that these are called the three *root* poisons, and this is because all mental afflictions arise from these three. It can be worthwhile to spend some time investigating instances when we are unhappy and seeing if we can indeed link them back to one or a combination of these. I think you'll find that it's true.

The three poisons are an important concept worthy of further study and contemplation. It relates to the Buddha's theory behind why we experience suffering in our life. I explore the three poisons in more depth during our retreats and in my book on the three poisons.

It's important that we introduce mindfulness to this and into our decision making and cultivate the ability to make decisions and act in ways that lead us towards the three domains of wellbeing, and away from the three root poisons.

The Perfection of Conative Intelligence

What does the *perfection* of conative intelligence look like? On a day-to-day basis, an individual with conative intelligence is able to observe desires as they come up in the mind, before they turn into behaviour, and is able to choose which ones to adopt and which ones to release, based on their potential end outcomes.

But how do we know which ones to choose and which ones to release? First of all, we do this by being mindful of what our highest aspirations are, of what kind of life we want to lead, of what is a meaningful life for us, and asking ourselves, "OK, this thought pattern has arisen. If I follow this thought pattern and it becomes a behaviour or an action, where will it take me?" For example, let's say we have a wellbeing, gym or meditation class, to attend. The thought arises, "'I'm not sure I can be bothered tonight." We consider occasions when we've engaged with this thought, action, or behaviour in the past, and recall where it took us. Perhaps in the past, you followed this through and skipped the class. This initially felt like a relief because we gave into that discomfort, and found some comfort. Later on, however, perhaps we felt some regret, and wished we had gone. We know it is good for us, and something we wanted to do. Because we skipped one, we felt behind and like we couldn't go back. We find ourselves back at square one, stuck and not making progress as we'd like to. We weigh up our past experience and try to imagine if we engaged in it now, where will it take me? Importantly, asking, "Will it bring me closer to my aspirations? Will it bring me closer to the life that I want?" That should be enough to awaken self-awareness and conative intelligence, but we could also take it further and ask, "OK, will it manifest in unhappiness, stress, or anxiety later on? Will it cause disharmony in my relationships?"

Having the wisdom to follow only those desires which are going to be beneficial to ourselves and others is very meaningful and powerful. If everyone managed to do this, there would be no cheating, no stealing, no killing, and harmony and peace would be the norm. If we have some understanding of karma and rebirth, conative intelligence is also about knowing what desires and intentions lead to happiness beyond this life and what will actually lead to suffering in future lives.

We could summarise leading a meaningful and deliberate life into a four step process:

1. Know what your aspirations are and what constitutes a meaningful life.
2. Understand what leads to your own and others' happiness.
3. Being mindful of your aspirations and what leads to genuine happiness.
4. Being mindful of our daily choices.

Know what your aspirations are and what constitutes a meaningful life

The first step is to be very clear on what our aspirations are for our life and what we feel constitutes a meaningful life. We should take some time to really consider this, having explored the section on genuine wellbeing and happiness. A meditation called the *Four-Fold Vision Quest* follows this section which will help you answer these questions. I recommend taking some time to contemplate and even write out your answers to these four questions. It can also help to contemplate them on a regular basis, cultivating strong awareness of them.

Understand what leads to your own and others' happiness

The second step is to understand what leads to our own and others' happiness. This can be about cultivating a self-awareness of the types of usual habits and behaviours we engage in and where they often take us. It is also about cultivating self-awareness of genuine happiness and wellbeing vs "quick wins" and stimulus-based pleasure, which as we've seen, is unsatisfactory and impermanent in nature.

Being mindful of your aspirations and what leads to genuine happiness

The third step is to be mindful of these first two; our aspirations, and what leads to genuine happiness. This means regularly keeping these in mind so that we are aware of them subconsciously. One such way to do this is to review and remember our aspirations and what constitutes a meaningful life for us every morning. The practice of aspiration setting and gratitude practices have been shown to have a very positive effect on our wellbeing. It helps remind us of our direction in life and keep us feeling motivated and positive. Being mindful of our aspirations does not mean we need to repeat them all day every day, similar to the bread example previously mentioned – when we know that we need to get bread on the way home, we're not thinking, "I need to get bread, I need to get bread, I need to get bread", over and over all day. If it's important to us that we have bread, then we will remember it on our way home. Likewise, if we know very clearly what our aspirations for our life are and what we feel is a meaningful life, and we know deep down what leads to our own and others' happiness and we put value and emphasis on that, then it will be easy and natural to be mindful of them, which brings us to step four.

Being mindful of our daily choices

Step four is to be mindful of our daily choices. A tip here is to introduce mindful moments to your day through your meditation practice and through regular present-centring. This will help you avoid going through your day mindlessly, which is where you run the risk of making decisions without checking in with yourself and being mindful of the long-term implications.

What is the knock-on effect? By engaging in these four simple steps, we'll see a ripple effect in our whole life. This way of being will quite literally impact everything. Our relationships will become more harmonious, our work or study will benefit, and our overall sense of happiness, wellbeing, and purpose will increase. There's no part of our life that won't be affected by us making more conatively intelligent choices.

This is not about avoiding doing fun things in life; this is solely about making a shift in our priorities. Instead of prioritising some of these quick wins, which feel nice at the time but have knock-on effects on our wellbeing, it's about prioritising what truly matters. It's also not about what someone else says truly matters; it's about for you, "What matters to me? What's my aspiration? What's a meaningful life for me? What really has a positive impact on my life and on my wellbeing? What is really going to lead me to where I want to be?" It's about prioritising your priorities. Because that's what you truly want when you say you want something better.

As mentioned before, the simple act of watching Netflix or eating ice cream, for example, isn't bad. Buying something for yourself isn't bad from its own side. These things are not conatively *un*intelligent things to do. The main thing is that we understand deep down that the lasting happiness we seek doesn't come from the TV, or from buying something for ourselves, or from the wine, but it actually comes from the three domains of wellbeing. It comes from within. The choices we make are only unwise if they're going to give rise to suffering for ourselves or others, and they will only give rise to suffering later from one of two ways: if we've misunderstood them and thought they were actually a cause of happiness because then we'll experience some frustration or disappointment. Or they'll give rise to suffering if that action is going to have a negative impact on those avenues of genuine wellbeing, like our ethics – the non-violent, benevolent way of life, or our mental balance – our calm, healthy state of mind. Conative intelligence is not about renouncing everything we have and all the nice things that we experience and saying, "these are unwise things to do" , but instead, it's about prioritising what really matters for us and prioritising our aspirations for a meaningful life.

Guided Meditation:
Four-Fold Vision Quest 🎧

To make a first leap towards leading a meaningful and deliberate life through conative intelligence, here is a practice designed to help you with step one - knowing clearly what your aspirations are for your life and what constitutes a meaningful life for you. This meditation is called the *Four-Fold Vision Quest* and is one I was introduced to by Lama Alan. Whether you feel you are aware of your highest aspirations or not, I would encourage you to enter into this practice with a completely fresh mindset, without any preconceived ideas, and allow the contemplation and understanding to come from some deeper level within.

Find a comfortable posture in which you can be quite relaxed and still. Relax into this posture and take some time to settle. Bring awareness to any areas of the body that feel tight or tense and release that tension with the outbreath.

If you find it helpful, take several significant and purposeful breaths. Fully inhale, expanding the belly and chest as much as you can, hold it for a moment, and exhale gently, feeling a wave of relaxation sweep over you.

Quiet the mind, settle it into the mode of simple witnessing. Release all concerns about the future and the past. Let your awareness rest in stillness in the present moment; still and clear.

For a short while, practice mindfulness of breathing to settle the mind further and bring it into a state of ease and focus

To begin the Four-Fold Vision Quest, we consider the first vision – your vision of your own flourishing. What does your greatest happiness and fulfilment look like? What would bring you the greatest sense of meaning? What would make you truly happy?

Try not to intellectually force an answer but feel into the practice and see what comes up from a deeper part of your being. It's okay if this vision isn't fully clear. Once you feel you have a vision, then with each outbreath, arouse the aspiration of loving-kindness that you may indeed realise your own fulfilment and highest joy. Manifest your heart's desire that you may be truly well and happy with every outbreath. As you breathe out, let it be as if you're breathing life into this vision; imagine realising here and now such well-being. Let your imagination play and draw that vision into the present moment and imagine it to be true here and now.

To realise such fulfilment, you cannot possibly do it on your own with no help. For your second vision, ask yourself what you would love to receive in the world around you. What would you love to see from the world around you? What would enable you to realise your highest ideals and greatest happiness?

With each inbreath, arouse the aspiration that it may be so. Arouse the wish that you may receive all that you truly need; that the world may rise up to meet you and fulfil your every need so that you may realise your highest ideals. Once again, let your imagination play and imagine receiving the kindness of your fellow sentient beings around you.

For your third observation, recognise that there's no possible way you can realise such fulfilment and awakening without bringing about very deep and irreversible inner transformation and maturation. Ask yourself how you would love to transform. How would you love to grow and mature? From what qualities would you love to be free? With what qualities would you love to be richly imbued in?

Let your imagination play. With every outbreath, arouse the aspiration: May it be so. With every outbreath, breathe life into this aspiration that it may come true. Imagine this becoming true here and now.

For our final observation, you once again recognise that you do not exist in isolation. The very fabric of your existence here is interwoven with all of those around you. It is a world of interdependence. In order to bring the greatest possible meaning to your own life and the greatest possible sense of fulfilment and satisfaction, consider what you would like to offer to the world. Drawing on your own unique background, interests, and abilities, what would you love to offer to the world around you? What are the greatest goods you can imagine sharing with the world to bring about the greatest possible benefit?

Imagine it. With every outbreath, arouse the aspiration: May it be so. Imagine offering here and now the greatest good you can imagine – to alleviate the suffering of the world, to help others. Imagine being a Buddha, a perfectly awakened one alleviating the suf-

fering of the world and bringing every sentient being to their own perfection.

Release all appearances and aspirations and let your awareness be still. Rest with the simple tactile experience of the body before bringing your practice to a close.

Questions and Responses

Question: Can I just ask, you said about the three domains of happiness, and then unhappiness. I got the first one – I think it was stimulus-dependent – but what was the next thing that you said? And could you explain more about the stimulus-dependent unhappiness that is actually caused by something within?

Answer: Yes, that is the two types of unhappiness. There is stimulus-dependent, and stimulus-independent. Stimulus-independent is that unhappiness that can seem to fester and bubble up from within, and we don't really know what the cause is or where it's coming from. To unpack that second part of your question, in our life, we experience unhappiness that appears to be caused by the external world, either as things that go wrong, or when we experience things that we don't want to experience, or when we are thwarted in our pursuit of some desire, and we don't get what we want. When this happens, we experience all manner of sufferings, whether it's frustration, disappointment, or downright misery and anger. It seems very logical to blame these emotional experiences and sufferings on the external event itself. But the key thing here is that there is actually a lot going on between the external event and the emotional response; we're just not aware of it. If there was nothing else going on between external event and emotional response, everyone would react the same, but every individual person has a different response to external challenge and change, and that is why some can be quite practical and joyful when they experience difficulties, and others quite frustrated and upset.

Question: So, this comes down to the individual person. But how can we change that and become the one who responds in a practical and joyful way?

Answer: That is a really great question, and I love getting down to the practicals. Of course, healing our neuroses and ingrained habits must take a very comprehensive and holistic approach. A combination of meditation, mindfulness practice, cultivating self-awareness, and so on. Specifically here though, how to work on our emotional responses, the process of the emotional episode timeline can be split into five stages, and I won't go into too much detail here, because to really unpack this well takes the entirety of our *Becoming Bulletproof: Emotional Resilience programme*, but I will explain it briefly. How the emotional episode plays out is influenced by a bunch of different things: our state of mind prior to it, our motivations and aspirations, whether the external event is a hot trigger for us, or if we have an ingrained habitual reaction; then, in the affect program there are all sorts of physiological and psychological changes, and eventually, there is either an automatic reaction based on uncontrolled habit, which is our norm, or there is an informed response, which comes from our being self-aware of how our emotions work, what our triggers are, and picking up on physiological and psychological cues in order to influence the episode before it becomes a destructive one. It's all about cultivating self-awareness and pausing when we become aware that we've become triggered. This pause can be very powerful. Viktor Frankl, the Austrian psychologist, and Holocaust survivor said: "'Between stimulus and response, there is a space. In that space is our power to choose our response. In our response lies our growth and our freedom." I think that sums it up very well.

Question: When we do the meditations ourselves and we start the meditation, would you start with a quick body scan and then go to the breath – as you do it with the guided meditations – and just keep returning to the sensations of the breath?

Answer: Yes, exactly. I would recommend doing it in exactly the same way I introduced here. There's this practice called settling body, speech, and mind in their natural states, which is what we did briefly first, prior to turning our attention to our breathing. I would encourage you to get quite familiar with this practice, and there is a free recording of that on the Samādhi Podcast if you want to do that separately. I personally always do this, settling body, speech, and mind in their natural states first. I found that if you just go straight into the mindfulness of breathing, we're not relaxed enough, we're still tense, we're quite fidgety, and we really need to cultivate that relaxation and stillness. So, it really helps to get ourselves in that right space. If we're not familiar with the settling body, speech, and mind practice, we might want to take our time with it. Perhaps our whole meditation consists of just that, but, as we become really familiar with it – and you only really need to do it for several days in a row to become quite familiar with it – then you'll be able to settle your body in its natural state quite quickly, then the speech, then the mind, quite naturally, so it becomes shorter and shorter. So yes, I would definitely go with that first. Also, a lot of people find it beneficial to have some sort of ritual to get them in the right headspace – maybe you light a couple of candles or incense, you clean the area, make the room nice and cosy, whatever helps get you into that mindset: "now I'm going into my practice". It's not necessary, but it helps some people get more relaxed and focused.

Question: I think I am someone who struggles with aversion. I do easily get angry with others and with life, and people at work. I seem to be someone who always has something going wrong. How can I stop being so angry?

Answer: Well, firstly, you've recognised the source of your anger as aversion. This is wonderful. Normally, we're pointing outwards, "I'm angry, who did this to me?" We find someone or something to blame, and then they become our target of frustration. So, first of all, recognising that the arising of anger has less to do with what has happened or what someone has said, and more to do with our way of responding. It's more about how we grab hold of what has happened and repeat the story to ourselves, what it means, why they did it, and exaggerate the events and significance of it. This creates a disturbance in the mind. When we're in traffic, for example, we get stuck in rejecting the situation. This is aversion. We may blame other road users, the things or people that delayed us at home, and get angry with them. We may get lost in worrying about the consequences of being late. This creates more disturbance. Instead of practically handling the situation, by taking another route or calling ahead, for example, we get stuck in our wanting the situation to be different. This is what aversion does. Exaggerates and perpetuates a situation, believing it to be inherently difficult. How do we overcome this? The Buddha teaches many ways, one such practical way is the teaching of patience. Patience means to accept wholeheartedly whatever arises, having given up the idea that things should be other than what they are. If we take our time to consider what that means, it simply means to let go of the version of events we want to happen and to accept what is actually happening in reality. In our traffic example, it is to let go of any "shoulds" or rigid beliefs we're holding on to, any "I should be there, I shouldn't be here", "this person shouldn't have moved my keys", "I shouldn't be late", and to wholeheartedly accept, "OK, I am in traffic. This is what is happening in my life". Patient acceptance doesn't mean you love what is happening, or that you agree with it; it simply means you give up your belief that it should be different. You said you seem to always have something going wrong in your life. This is because you see these events as being wrong, and attach stories and significance to them, instead of accepting they are what they are. As a first step, if you can recognise that "wrong" and "right" are simply mental concepts and not a quality of the event themselves, then you make dealing with challenge easier. Being able to do this is liberating and opens the doorway to inner peace and practical thinking. If we get lost in anger, the best part of our brain and mind fail to function. With patient acceptance, we can remain calm in the midst of challenge and change and deal with the situation with a practical, creative mind.

Meditation Skills:
Relaxation is Key

Our meditation practice is an essential foundation for us to be able to cultivate mindfulness in these other four areas that we're exploring because it gives us a bit of a calm space in the day and counteracts chronic distractibility, turbulence, and noise. With a regular time out in the day, we'll find it easier to introduce awareness into the rest of our day. We'll be able to introduce awareness into what's going on in the mind and what's going on in the body. We're also training our mindfulness, which will benefit other areas of our life. The stronger our mindfulness, the easier it will be to concentrate when we need to, to live deliberately, to be in the present moment, to be mindful when we're eating, and to be mindful of the mind, thoughts, and so on.

I would like now to introduce a couple of different concepts or tools that can help improve our meditation on mindfulness of breathing. Mindfulness of breathing was the approach that the Buddha himself strongly emphasised, and in particular, for this approach, we're drawing from the writings of Asanga, who was an Indian scholar and Mahayana master of the 4th century. In this method, we are attending to the entire breathing body: all the sensations we experience related to the breath; the *prana*, the vibration, the tingling of all kinds – not just in the abdomen, or in the chest, or the nostrils – but throughout the entire body, the legs, and the arms, and into the head as well. As we attend closely to the body as we breathe, we start to notice all sorts of subtle movements throughout the body that are related to the rhythm of the breath. All these sensations are included in this first mode, and in particular, this way of attending to the breath is really conducive to relaxation, and a lot of us are not very good at relaxation.

For this meditation, I really want you to emphasise relaxation and get as relaxed and loose as possible. To do that, you need to be very comfortable. So please choose a posture that is comfortable for you and will minimise fidgeting. Also implicit in this meditation is a balancing act; we need to cultivate an ever-deepening sense of relaxation throughout the entire session, relaxing more and more, but without losing the level of clarity and wakefulness that you have right now as you read this book.

Three Qualities of Successful Meditation

In shamatha meditation, there are three qualities that we're trying to cultivate, and they can be likened to a pyramid. It starts with relaxation at its foundation. Upon that relaxation is stability, and upon that stability, at the apex, is clarity. You need all three to succeed in meditation. Without these three qualities, your meditation experience will be one of distraction or sleepiness. If you try and go straight for the clarity – which is what many people do – by focusing really closely on, for example, the nostrils, and really try and have that vividness, you find that you cause problems for yourself. You get hyper vigilant, especially if you try and do it for long periods of time if you haven't brought relaxation first. In his book, *The Attention Re-*

volution, Lama Alan describes the relationship among these three as "like the roots, the trunk and the foliage of a tree". As your practice grows, the roots of relaxation go deeper, the trunk of stability gets stronger, and the foliage of the vividness and clarity reaches higher. Overall, following the sage advice of the contemplatives before us, that's what we're aiming to cultivate. For this session, I encourage you to solely focus on this quality of relaxation, without losing the wakefulness and clarity with which you are starting. As we engage in this meditation, we will utilise two tools:

Noting the Rhythm of the Breath

First, following the teachings of the Buddha directly, we will introduce a layer to the practice where we simply note the duration of the breath. To paraphrase the Buddha's pith instructions: on the occasions where the breath flows in and it is long, we note that it is long. When the outbreath is long, we note that it is long. And on occasion, the inbreath is bound to be relatively short, so we note that it is short. And when the outbreath is short, we note that it is short.

These are the Buddha's first four instructions of his sixteen phases of mindfulness of breathing practice. This is the first layer we will add to our meditation, and we simply note the duration of the breath, moment to moment. Crucially, this noting the rhythm is not about attending to the whole breath and then conceptually considering its length with such thoughts as "hmm, that was short, was it slightly shorter than the last one?" It is not about conceptualising or thinking about it, but it's a more natural flow of knowing. When you hear a dog bark, you know it's a dog without having to say or specifically think "dog". By the time you have said or thought "dog" your mind has already known the phenomena and moved on. When we are attending to the breath, we simply take enough interest to know whether the breath is long or short, without having to conceptualise it.

Mindfulness & Introspection

As a meditator on the path of shamatha, we are primarily training two faculties of mind. The first is mindfulness, whose job is to hold the breath single-pointedly without forgetfulness. The second tool is the mental faculty of introspection, a translation of the Sanskrit *samprajanya*. This is the part of the mind that checks up and monitors your body, speech, and mind, not only during meditation but at all times. In meditation, its job is quality control. First, it checks the body, "Am I still in a good posture? Have I fallen over?" Secondly, it checks our state of mind and the flow of mindfulness itself, "Am I falling asleep? Have I become distracted?" We utilise introspection now and again to check in with ourselves to see if we're still focusing on the breath, to ensure the breath is still natural, that our posture is good, and that we are still focused on the breath. These two faculties of mindfulness – holding the object, moment to moment – and our introspection – checking up, saying, "look, you got distracted" – are the two mental faculties active during our meditation and that we are carefully training.

When you do notice that you become distracted, what do you do? The solution here is not to tense up or to become tighter, or more frustrated, but instead it is to relax. So, when you notice your mind wandering, react by first relaxing your body, relaxing your mind, then release the distraction with the outbreath, and return to the breath. Your job is to keep doing that as many times as you need to. Every time you get distracted, just keep doing it: relax, release, return. If you notice that you've become sleepy, dull, tired, then your response should be to refresh your interest, restore your attention and retain it as best you can.

Guided Meditation: Mindfulness of Breathing - Focus on Relaxation 🎧

Find a comfortable posture in which you can be quite relaxed and still. If you are seated, use the seven-point meditation posture, and if you are lying down, then use the shavasana. Your eyes may be closed or partially open. Relax into this posture and take some time to settle. Set the intention to remain as still as possible for this meditation. Bring to mind your most meaning-

ful aspiration for this practice so that it may be of benefit to yourself and others.

To begin the practice, let your awareness once again descend down to those sensations of the earth element where your body is in contact with the chair, the cushion, or the floor. Try to quiet the mind and settle it into the mode of simple witnessing. This is a non-verbal witnessing presence. Once you feel grounded and settled, let your awareness fill and permeate the whole space of your body, immediately experiencing what it is like to be embodied, to experience this physical body from the inside.

And as you maintain a mindful presence throughout the body, set your body at ease. Relax the muscles of the shoulders and surrender your muscles to gravity. Bring awareness to the face and soften the muscles around the eyes, the mouth, the jaw, and the area around the temples. Let the forehead feel spacious and open, with no contraction whatsoever, the same between the eyebrows.

Allow the body to breathe effortlessly, fully releasing the breath, without forcefully expelling it but without retaining any. With every outbreath relax more *in the body, releasing any tension, relaxing the muscles, and releasing any thoughts which may be trying to captivate your attention, allowing them to dissolve back into the mind. Breathe as effortlessly as if you were deep asleep.*

Let your prana system balance itself out.

Set aside any hopes, concerns, or thoughts about the past, present, or the future. Release all expectations and all grasping, and let your awareness come to rest in the present moment, fully aware of the body.

While resting in this stillness of your awareness, observe the movements throughout the body, in particular the movements of prana; this energetic flow, vibration, tingling, and movements of all kinds.

Among the many sensations you can feel throughout the body, you'll begin to note these rhythmic sensations that are clearly associated with the flow of your breath. This is not only the rise and fall of the abdomen, the expansion of the diaphragm, sensations in the chest, or the nostrils, but attend closely and you may sense fluctuations of energy in your legs, throughout your torso, throughout your arms, and up into your head. Selectively focus on those fluctuations throughout the entire body that are correlated with the in and the out flow of the breath.

To help us maintain an ongoing sense of knowing and attend to every inhalation and every exhalation, we can follow the instructions of the Buddha himself. On those occasions where the breath flows in and it is long, note that it is long.

When the outbreath is long, note that it is long. On occasion, the inbreath is bound to be relatively short as we become relaxed; note that it is short. When the outbreath is short, note that it is short.

Now and again utilise your introspection, noticing when laxity or excitation has set in and taking appropriate action. Also, with introspection check up on your posture and see that you remain relaxed, still, and vigilant.

Before closing the meditation, dedicate the positive energy or merit that you've generated to your highest aspirations and intentions. Close with a few words of loving-kindness and compassion, such as "May all beings find happiness and the causes of happiness. May all beings be free of suffering and the causes of suffering."

3 - Stop Living in Our Imagination

Life doesn't just happen to us. We choose the kind of life we want to lead with our thoughts and our actions, and our thoughts and our actions don't have to be out of control. With mindfulness, we cultivate the ability to stop following along blindly with whatever the mind wants to do, reconnect with our innate power to choose and start wielding that power.

I believe many of us are spending a huge amount of our time in our imagination. Imagination is not just for kids, but it's something that a lot of us as adults are engaging in regularly. Whether we spend a lot of our time ruminating about things in the future, such as the things that will happen or things we'd like to happen, planning the next meal, the next meeting, or worrying about the outcomes of our choices, or even dreaming about running away and winning the lottery. Perhaps we find that we have a tendency to always go over the past; our traumas, things that went wrong, our resentments, guilt, shame, and anger about what has happened. All of these activities are happening in the mental domain, and if they're up in the mental domain, then they're not actually happening here and now in the physical reality that's being presented to us. Thoughts about the past or the future are rarely in touch with reality.

We may think that thoughts about the past are reality based because they are about events that have happened. If I'm remembering something that has happened, then it's real, not imagination. However, even this is imagination based. First of all, we're remembering our perspective. We often believe that our perception is 100% a true account of what happened. We were there, we should know. But our perspective and our perception at any given moment is clouded by various things: our physical viewpoint, our mental state, our triggers, our attachments, our aversions, our emotions, our opinions, and beliefs, and is not as pure a vision as we believe. As we then recall a memory today, it's further filtered by today's views, opinions, beliefs, mental state, attachments, and so on. Every time we recall a memory, it changes ever so slightly. We focus selectively on a certain portion of it: how it felt to be embarrassed, or the way they said what they said. By focusing on and noticing only certain parts of a memory, it gets more weight, it gets more focus and becomes more significant.

For example, if we recall an altercation with our partner, and find ourselves fixated on the way our partner said the word "no", we may find ourselves lost in thoughts such as "they said 'no' in a really strange way, I wonder what they meant by that? They seemed really upset. Maybe they don't like me anymore. Maybe they're tired of me. I push everyone away". By engaging with this memory in this way, we've inadvertently put a lot of weight on a particular point and it has become wildly exaggerated and unrealistic. We're engaging only with our perspective, which is filtered over and over again and becomes twisted and does not tell a whole story. Because of this, it changes over time as well. Every time we remember something and go back to that memory, it changes slightly. The other individual will also have an entirely different memory!

Recalling memories can feel like we're living in that moment again, experiencing the scenario detail by detail, when really what we're doing is using our present emotions and state of mind as an anchor to describe the past. While we're remembering, our imagination fills in all the gaps for us. This means that we're only actively remembering a small part, and our imagination is filling in the rest. Often, two people can talk about a memory, and it's totally a different story, or they disagree over who said what. Both people swear that they remember it exactly how it happened, and so, who is right? The memory they're seeing is a creation of the mind; it's a mix of their perception of what happened and a whole host of filters, emotions, and imagination. It is out of touch with reality. The same goes with our future.

It's not difficult to see how our imagination is at play when we're thinking about the future. Humans are very creative. We're great at fantasizing about the future, and we're also very good at creating worst-case scenarios. Many of us think and worry about the future relentlessly, imagining the implications of our decisions, how we're going to feel when this happens, how we're going to feel after a nice meal, or why our partner isn't answering our text messages. All of these thoughts about the future are predictions which, actually, the majority of the time, are not helpful to us. On an evolutionary level, human imagination has been very useful in helping us predict dangers and has aided survival. For most nowadays, however, rejection by a partner does not really affect our chances of survival, but this doesn't stop our hyperactive creative mind from taking over and predicting all sorts of weird and wonderful outcomes. This happens because we believe our partner to be a source of our happiness and joy, and we can't bear to lose our happiness. If we knew the true nature of mind and genuine happiness, however, then we wouldn't fear loss.

Sometimes it can feel good to revel in what might be, imagining what our future might look like when we get this job, and we have a bit more money, or when we finally move into a new home. We see it turning out well, and we look forward to it, but it's easy to see how this can go wrong sometimes. If we're overly optimistic and we set expectations on events unfolding just the way we imagine it, and then it doesn't, we're unhappy or disappointed. Getting a new job, going on holiday, or moving into a new home is not the problem. The expectation that these things will bring us that lasting happiness and fulfilment we've been looking for is the problem. We often fail to realise that the root cause of our unhappiness is due to these overly ambitious expectations that we set on our world and other people. The disappointment came not from the event but from our expecting it to be other than what it was. If we're constantly fantasising about the future and how it's going to turn out, how our partner is going to do this for us, how we're going to get this place, then when that doesn't happen, we've set ourselves up for disappointment, because we've expected it to be one way and not another.

Based on our above analysis, it's fair to say that we're spending a lot of our time out of touch with the reality that's happening right in front of us. We normally have diagnoses for those who are out of touch with reality, but, actually, from this perspective, most of us are out of touch with reality, and many of us are mentally unwell.

Of course, we are unable to abide completely in the present moment every minute of every day – looking and planning ahead and reflecting on the past are at times necessary activities. However, we needn't spend as much time there as we do, especially when we are tormenting ourselves, and we may find benefit from being more present and spending less time in our imagination. Abraham Maslow said that the ability to be in the present moment is a major component of mental wellness. Indeed, we can only achieve and experience genuine happiness, peace, and joy in the present moment. Just like watching the breath, it's impossible to experience the breath in the future or the past, just like we cannot experience genuine happiness in the future or the past now. The only time you are able to experience is right now, and our ability to be in the present moment is key to our mental well-being.

Two Points about the Dangers of Not Living in the Present Moment

To be able to start living more in the present moment, we need the motivation to do so. To bring about this motivation, we need to realise what are the problems and the dangers associated with not living in the present moment.

The Future Is Not Under Our Control

The first point to contemplate is that the future is not under our control, and this moment that we're experiencing right now is the only moment that we can really control. We can influence the future, of course, but actual control is an illusion. We can't control what's going to happen in a year's time, or in two years; we barely have control over the next five minutes. I can decide to go and make myself a cup of tea right now, but there's no guarantee that my water hasn't been shut off, or that my power stops working. There are no guarantees beyond the small things that we can influence with our intention and actions. Even those things, however, we can only influence right now in the present moment and not in the future.

By living in the present moment, we stop trying to guess what might or might not happen in the future, and instead, we stay focused on what's happening in the here and now. When we do this, we find that the connection between our awareness, our body, and our mind is restored. They all come together, working in harmony. With that comes a balance, a dynamic equilibrium, in which there is mental peace, emotional balance, and a reality-based outlook. With all three of these in sync, we alleviate much of the anxiety and the stress that's caused by our thinking about the past or thinking about the future. Being present helps us feel a lot calmer, a lot more at peace.

Life Unfolds in Moments

The second point to consider is that life only unfolds in moments. Because life happens in moments, the best way to handle things that come our way is to take things one moment at a time. An interesting truth here is that 99% of the moments of our day are actually good – nothing is going wrong, all is well, we have our comforts, and we can be at peace. For 99% of our day, the moment itself is good, but we can actually ruin a whole day or a whole week by thinking or stressing about something that is coming in the future.

This was a problem that I personally always used to have. I would have this recurring work meeting that would come up on Mondays and Fridays. Because of my hyperactive focus on what was coming in the future, most of my Sunday would be ruined because I would be ruminating and worrying about this meeting: what they're going to say, how they're going to say it, how they were finally ready to just fire me – all these kinds of thoughts. I would let my whole Sunday be consumed by this way of thinking, stressing about what was going to happen at that meeting. Then during the week as well, every time that meeting crossed my mind, or every time that client's name popped up in an email, I'd start thinking and worrying about that one thing.

As life unfolded in moments on that Sunday, I could have just enjoyed my day. I could have just done and enjoyed whatever I wanted to do: going for a walk, spending time with family, enjoying a film, a wander around a museum, or a walk on the beach. Instead, I allowed what was going to be 15 or 30 minutes of a stressful situation, to ruin an entire Sunday day and night, a whole Monday morning, and so many other days and nights that I've lost from worrying about that situation. By attending to this future event in this way, I was extending 15 minutes of pain into days or weeks of pain, and that was all self-inflicted.

When we turn those 15 minutes into a whole week of worry, stress, or anxiety, it doesn't just destroy our mental peace, but it stops us from just enjoying the moments we have. It also affects our physical health too – our sleep, our energy levels, our overall mood, which affects our relationships with others. All because we weren't just living presently, enjoying and being with the moments that were unfolding before us. The vast majority of those moments were all good in themselves without past or future imagination involved.

Perhaps one of the worst parts is that despite my significant investment of time and energy into this worrying and rumination, it actually had very little influence on the outcome of the meetings themselves. My worrying didn't make the meeting go away, nor did it change what was going to happen; its only function was self-inflicted pain.

Attempting to constantly try to solve our entire life in one instance brings on so much unnecessary anxiety and distracts us from what is actually happening in front of us. It is much more beneficial for us to focus our time and our energy on each moment as it comes. It's the only reality we have, and as we see, the vast majority of these moments are actually OK.

We Can Enjoy Pleasant Circumstances and Overcome Unpleasant Circumstances

By living in the present moment, we start to let go of the grasping and clinging onto what we think our life should be or how it should turn out. With no expectations of the future, we won't be as disappointed or as devastated by the things that happen and the things that do go wrong. Instead, we will go into life with a flexible, open mind, with no expectations of how our day is going to go, just openly, wholeheartedly, willing to accept and deal with whatever comes – good or bad.

By living in this way, we can enjoy the good things and pleasant circumstances more, because we're not clinging onto them with thoughts of "don't go away" or "don't leave me". Instead, we can just enjoy them, and just be present with them. Sometimes good experiences can be tainted by the afflictions of craving and attachment because we hold on to things as being quite fixed, permanent, and as being sources of happiness from their own side. An understanding of impermanence and living in the present moment counteracts this and means we can just enjoy what is happening and not be disappointed when it ends, or cling on so much for the next best thing.

On the other hand, when things go wrong, we can also recognise that these things too are impermanent and unfold moment by moment. We have a tendency when something goes wrong for us, to solidify and reify that difficulty. There's a part of us that thinks that this suffering is quite permanent, solid, and unchanging and that we can't and don't want to experience it, then we instantly reject it. This firm rejection brings on the stress and the tension we experience, as we struggle to let go of that which we think should happen and come to terms with what is actually happening. If we were to recognise that just like everything else, it will unfold moment by moment, and actually, this challenge is not something solid and unchanging but is something that will pass, then we may feel up to the task. I often think that if challenges came with a big sign that told us in advance how long it would last, "I'm a 10 minute inconvenience", or "I'm a one hour challenge", that with the comfort of knowing that it will pass and an understanding that we have the strength and resilience to handle it, challenges would be overcome with a much calmer and more open heart and mind. If we knew how long the difficulty would last and let go of our belief that we shouldn't experience difficulties, the resolve "I can deal with that" would arise naturally. We'd see that this is a small patch in the tapestry of our week, and an even smaller patch on the tapestry of our life, and we have the inner strength and resilience because we've dealt with much worse in the past.

The truth is, that despite how it seems, difficulties are finite, and with a 100% success rate of getting through our bad days, there's nothing we cannot handle. As Jack Kornfield says:

> "We start to realise our hearts are big enough. We come back to the vastness, we come back to this perspective of not blaming and judging, we come back to a place of trusting that the heart can hold it all."

We Make the Most of Every Moment

By staying present, we stop comparing how our life used to be, or how it could be. It can be nice to dream about the future: when things will be better, when the pandemic is over, when we have improved health, a new job, more money, a happier life. The flip side of this is that we tend to put our life on hold. We miss out on the very fact that we are living right here, right now. This is the life we have. This is the moment we have. If we're waiting for something to come in the future, then we're wasting this moment, which turns into wasted days and wasted weeks. It appears that many people have been doing this in the lockdowns of 2020 and 2021; putting their life on hold and thinking there's nothing they can do. Each moment has potential, and it is up to us to use it. We can be utilising every moment towards our vision of a meaningful life. That is an incredibly powerful and liberating way to be, to utilise every moment and recognise that all we ever experience is this moment here. Positive qualities of mind such as acceptance, gratitude, compassion, and kindness naturally arise when we're living in the present moment – which improves our way of being and our relationships. We live with less worry, less anxiety, and we start to become more productive as well.

Living in the present moment and attending to what you're doing is a quality of concentration. Have you ever noticed how productive and how good you can feel when you turn off all distractions and just fully engage with the task at hand? Whether it's work, study, reading, or engaging in a hobby, when you're in the zone, everything becomes so much easier. Your ideas flow better, your problem solving is better, your creative thinking is active, and when you feel like you're in the zone, it's effortless. What is "the zone"? It's concentration, it's present moment awareness, it's being completely absorbed in the activity; awareness, body, and mind, all in the same place, engaging in the same activity.

By allowing yourself to be fully present and engaged in what you're doing, first of all, things like work become a lot easier and you're a lot more productive, but you also find work more enjoyable. Many of us have a tendency to, while we're working or studying, put on music, or watch a video, juggle a lot of stimulus and tasks at the same time. There's research out there that shows that multitasking in this way is not healthy and is quite turbulent for our mind. You can feel the difference and relief sometimes when it comes to an end. It's like when you have loud music in the car on your way home, and then you park up and turn it all off, and you can almost feel some buzzing in your head and the silence is deafening.

By being present with what's going on, we'll find that we have a calmer, happier presence, able to enjoy anything we do because we're more aware of the experiences that are happening as well. For example, eating. We have a tendency to wolf down some food and don't even really think about it, but eating can actually be a whole experience – the taste, textures, aromas. Even the most mundane tasks like housework can be really therapeutic when we fully engage in our senses, in what is presenting to us, in what's happening in the body, in the mind, and you can become grateful for the smaller, simpler things in life.

How to Live in the Present Moment

I've spent a fair bit of time here in this chapter discussing the "why" behind living in the present moment and not in our imagination, and the whole point of this is to spur our own contemplation and reflection, which feeds into our motivation, our aspiration, and our enthusiasm for trying to live more in the moment. This is the key to unlocking the present moment.

Living in the present moment is a spectrum: it's not as simple as living mindfully or living unmindfully, and we make changes gradually over time. It's important not to shame ourselves for wherever we are on that spectrum. Instead, we cultivate the determination to move at least a little bit further towards mindful living, based on the benefits it can have for us.

For us to make that internal shift though, we need to look at our present habits and the way we go about our day, contemplate some of the issues we have and see if any are connected, caused, or exacerbated by spending too much time in the imagination, and cultivate a strong resolve to live differently. We want to come to the determination, "No, I'm not going to carry on with that same old habit. I know where it leads me. I know that it leads to feeling unbalanced, anxious, feeling worried. Instead, I'm going to focus on what's arising here and now".

Change begins with a deliberate act of will, with knowing "this is what I want to do" and making an effort to do it. The other ways and methods outlined in this book are designed to help us with living in the present moment. In chapter one, we were introduced to a body scan practice designed for present-centring. The moment you bring your awareness to the body or the breath and you're fully attentive with it, you are here in the present moment, because you can't attend to your breath in the future or in the past.

Motivation is Key

All of these changes and all spiritual practice starts with motivation. If we don't have the desire to give up the mundane, same old ways of feeling, experiencing the world, emotions, blockages, and limiting thoughts that we've experienced time and time again, if we're not fed up with those and want to live differently, we'll never do anything to change it.

If you have the motivation and the aspiration, then you can start to work on it. Just like with meditation, when you get a taste of what present-centred living can do for you, and you get a taste for the benefits and the inner wellbeing that you can tap into, from there comes a faith born out of confidence. Faith here doesn't mean some blind belief in something higher or in what someone tells you, but faith born out of confidence and our experience in the practice. This is the kind of faith you have when you get on a plane; you have faith in the pilot: confidence that he's had his training, that he knows what he's doing, that he knows how to fly, and he knows how to land. Faith in the engineers who built the plane. Faith you're going to be OK, that it's all going to go alright, and this is based on your understanding, your confidence, and your experience. So, with some experience of the practice, we'll start to get that faith in the practice. We'll get a sense that we've tapped into something quite special, some sort of inner wellbeing and genuine happiness. When our aspiration for living differently comes together with our faith in a particular practice, then arises enthusiasm, and from natural enthusiasm comes real progress. This can be compared to learning any skill, like piano or crocheting. When you first began, it was difficult. But with aspiration, and faith in your method of learning comes that enthusiasm. Once you hear something and it sounds good, the enthusiasm just naturally carries you and it's effortless. It is the same with meditation, present-centred living, and any other spiritual practice. Once we start to experience the benefits and we get a taste for it, we'll want more, and the enthusiasm will spur us on.

Guided Meditation: Loving-Kindness (Metta)

An important part of Buddhist meditation is the ongoing cultivation of the heart. An enlightened mind is not just the essence of wisdom but the union of wisdom and compassion. For this reason, the cultivation of the *Four Immeasurables* – loving-kindness, compassion, empathetic joy, and equanimity – are an essential part of the path. These immeasurable qualities enrich our spiritual practice and bring joy, love, and connection to our daily life.

Find a comfortable posture where you can be quite relaxed and still. You may choose to do this meditation seated or lying down. Relax into your chosen posture and take some time to settle. Bring to mind your most meaningful aspiration for this practice so that it may be of benefit to yourself and others.

Bring your awareness to the sensations of your body, breathing into areas that feel tense or constricted. Take three slow deep breaths, breathing through your nostrils and out through the mouth. Exhale effortlessly, settling the body in its resting state.

Attend to the rhythm of your breath for a few minutes. Release the worries of the day, release anticipations of the future, and settle into the only reality there is: the present moment.

Once you feel settled and grounded, begin the metta meditation by turning your attention to yourself, as you are here and now. Bring to mind your desire to find genuine happiness and the causes of genuine happiness. Also arouse the belief and the affirmation that you deserve to be happy, to live with ease, to be safe, and to be well.

Then, take your time to carefully recite the following phrases of loving-kindness, thinking about the meaning and feeling into the words:

May I live with ease,

May I be safe and healthy,

May I flourish and find genuine happiness.

Then, think of a person close to you who loves you very much. It could be someone from the past or the present, someone still in life or who has passed, and imagine that person standing in front of you, sending you their love. They are sending you wishes for your safety, wellbeing, and happiness. Allow yourself to feel the warm wishes and love coming from that person towards you.

Then imagine that you are surrounded on all sides by all the people who love you and have loved you. They are also sending you wishes for your happiness, wellbeing, and health. Bask in the warm wishes and *love coming from all sides. You are filled and overflowing with warmth and love.*

Next, we turn our attention to a very close friend, partner, or loved one. Bring to mind their specific desires and aspirations. Bring to mind their desire to be happy, and then wish them well. May their yearnings be fulfilled. May they find satisfaction.

Then, take your time to carefully recite the following phrases of loving-kindness, thinking about the meaning and feeling into the words:

May you live with ease,

May you be safe and healthy,

May you flourish and find genuine happiness.

The next phase of the practice is to focus on a neutral person, someone to whom you really don't give much thought one way or another. If you heard some news about them, your mind would basically remain unmoved. And arouse that wish once again. As for myself, so for you. You also wish to be free of suffering. You also wish to find happiness. May you experience it. Let the loving-kindness you felt for yourself and your friend slide over to the person towards whom you feel neutral.

Then, take your time to carefully recite the following phrases of loving-kindness, thinking about the meaning and feeling into the words:

May you live with ease,

May you be safe and healthy,

May you flourish and find genuine happiness.

For the final phase of the practice, direct your attention to a person with whom you have a difficult relationship. This could be someone to whom we feel some hostility or hatred. If there is no one in this category, this is wonderful, but if there is even so much as a politician who elicits these feelings in you, then turn your attention to them now.

Take some time to contemplate that this person, like you, desires happiness, and to be free of suffering. The way they pursue happiness may be wrong, and cause harm, but they too are victim to their mental afflictions, they succumb to anger, hatred, jealousy, and this makes them act in ways that bring them only suffering. They bring about their own suffering. There is a ray of light within this person; they too have the potential to be loving, kind people. They have people who love them; they are loved. Recognise that at their core, beneath it all, they are just like you; they desire happiness and freedom. Think "You also wish to be free of suffering. You also wish to find happiness. May you experience it".

Let the loving-kindness you feel for yourself, your friends, and loved ones, let it expand and encompass this person. Then, take your time to carefully recite the following phrases of loving-kindness, thinking about the meaning and feeling into the words:

May you also live with ease,

May you also be safe and healthy,

May you also flourish and find genuine happiness.

Before closing the meditation, dedicate the positive energy or merit that you've generated to your highest aspirations and intentions. Close with a few words of loving-kindness and compassion, such as "May all beings find happiness and the causes of happiness. May all beings be free of suffering and the causes of suffering".

Discussion: Questions and Responses

Question: I really liked this concept of the past and future being like imagination. I'm someone who spends a lot of time going over past experiences, and as you've been talking, I've been thinking about how accurate these thoughts are. I think they have become quite exaggerated, and I can see how I fill in the blanks. What you've said has really made me think about how I spend my time, and how it's not useful to go over things again and again. Thank you.

Response: Thank you. I think what you said at the end there is the key part: how useful is it? That's what it comes down to, right? How useful is this anyway? Sure, there are times we need to think ahead, to plan ahead, and there are times we need to recall the past, but how useful is it to go over that same story for the fifth time in five minutes? (Laughs).

The other side is not just "is it useful" but "is it harmful"? What is the short and long term effects on my wellbeing? Coming back to conative intelligence again - is it actually going to cause me some harm, disturb my peace of mind, affect my work, my time with my loved ones, and so on?

Question: Thank you for sharing the meditation on loving-kindness, I think this is really important. Do you think these *Four Immeasurables* can help with loneliness?

Response: Absolutely, without a doubt! Remember that being lonely is different from being alone. We can be quite happy and content in solitude – being physically alone – and we can be lonely even in a crowded room. So, loneliness is a state of mind, and it's caused by feeling disconnected, by feeling a lack of social fulfilment. In these times our view becomes quite narrow, focused on our sense of self and it being very separate from others. Imagine it as a closed bud of a flower, a lotus, closed off from everyone else. Loving-kindness and compassion are a way of turning our attention from inside the bud, to those outside the bud, seeing all these other beings out there that are just like me, and just like me they want to be happy and free of suffering, and I wish that for them, I really do.

Empathetic joy especially, is this way of attending to the good fortune, the virtue, the joy, the happiness there is out there, and sharing in that, taking delight in it. So, we might see a young couple together holding hands, or a group of friends together, and a miserly response might be envy or a feeling of "I wish I had that". Focusing on the inside of the bud again. Whereas empathetic joy, is like the blossoming of that lotus, opening up to others, looking to them, and thinking "how wonderful! I'm so glad they get to enjoy that". Taking delight in it and sharing in the happiness you see in their faces. Watching kids play, dogs and cats playing, friends reuniting, neighbours tending to their gardens, activists in our world doing good, volunteers helping others, and so on. So, the *Four Immeasurables* are a way of turning our attention, connecting with others on a mind level, and this squashes loneliness. I've heard the Dalai Lama say that if he focusses on himself as the Dalai Lama, as "I am only one", it's quite a lonely position. But he thinks of himself as one of seven billion others, all seeking the same thing. From that perspective, he is one of many, connected on this fundamental level.

Meditation Skills:
Enhancing Stability

Until now in our meditation skills training, we've been emphasising the first essential quality of relaxation. Progress in meditation is achieved not through tightening our mind at the expense of relaxation, but through easing more and deepening our relaxation as the meditation progresses. This approach helps us to release the energy around agitation. In the first mode, the Asanga approach to mindfulness of breathing is particularly emphasised. Focusing on the whole body breathing is a relaxing activity, much like watching waves wash upon shore. As we train our mental faculty of mindfulness, we also train our faculty of introspection. This is the part of the mind that my teacher often refers to as the "quality control". It is introspection's job to now and again monitor our body, our posture, our breathing, and the flow of mindfulness itself. It is the part of the mind that checks in and says "are we still focusing on the breath, or have I gotten distracted and I'm wandering? Am I falling asleep?", and so on. With effective introspection, we can then take the appropriate action to bring ourselves back on course.

From this sense of relaxation we have cultivated previously, we can now start to build some stability of attention, which is the second essential quality of meditation. Stability is about how long we can maintain our attention continuously on the object of meditation, in this case, the sensations of the breath.

It is important that we cultivate stability on the basis of relaxation. To begin our meditation, we focus initially on the relaxation element, but as the meditation progresses, we try to do so without losing the wakefulness with which we began.

The reason we build our stability upon the foundation of relaxation is because although we can make progress in meditation with sheer effort and grit, it's not sustainable. For example, we can make a very tight fist with our hand, but how long can we make a tight fist easily? Could you hold it for an hour, two hours, 24 hours? It would be very difficult to do so. Therefore, our practice needs to be rooted in a sense of ease and relaxation. Contrary to our typical western way of approaching skills development and achievements, we don't make progress in meditation by knuckling down thinking "I will meditate. I will focus on my object. I will achieve this. It'll all go amazing". Instead, we need to start with that sense of ease we've been practising.

One way to cultivate our quality of stability is to direct our attention downwards to the sensations in the abdomen – focusing on the whole belly – simply noticing the rise and the fall as we breathe in and breathe out. The Asanga approach of mindfulness of the entire body breathing is very helpful for relaxing the mind, but it's also easy to become relaxed and then become a bit dull or spaced out because the object is very obvious. But this technique of focusing on the abdomen, as commonly taught in the Burmese Theravada tradition, is really helpful for stabilising the mind. Like the whole body approach, the object is still quite coarse, so it won't take us all the way to the achievement of shamatha – meditative quiescence – but it's in no way a basic practice because it can get us all the way to the fourth stage of shamatha. At the fourth stage, we can be practising for an hour or more without becoming entirely disengaged from the object. This is an incredible achievement that can be realised just by attending to the belly going up and going down.

One of the reasons for exploring these different approaches to mindfulness of breathing is because each one suits a different person and at different times. Some people really find the belly approach to be very engaging, others prefer the whole body. This also changes as our attention skills improve. By trying these different approaches ourselves we find which one works for us right now. With direct first-hand experience, you'll have a repertoire of practices to use, so that when you're especially tense, you know a method that will work for you. When you are quite relaxed but want to cultivate your stability, then you will have a method to use.

Guided Meditation: Mindfulness of Breathing - Focus on Stability 🎧

For our next mode of mindfulness of breathing, we turn to a fairly recently devised method, which I've heard dates back only as early as the 19th century. This method is very helpful in stabilising the mind because it brings our attention down. When our mind is especially dominated by excitation, turbulence, and agitation, it can be useful to lower the focus of our attention and bring it down. If, on the other hand, our attention is dull or sleepy, then elevating the focus of our attention, up to the nostrils, for example, can be very helpful. There is a meditative technique called "switching gears" that follows a similar theory, which can be worth experimenting with. If you are especially distracted during your meditation, try tilting your head down slightly and see if it helps to calm the mind. If you're falling asleep or becoming spaced out or dull, you may notice that your head is naturally tipping forward, so try elevating your head slightly and see if it helps refresh your quality of attention.

Find a comfortable posture in which you can be quite relaxed and still. You may choose to do this meditation seated or lying down. Relax into your chosen posture and take some time to settle. Bring to mind your most meaningful aspiration for this practice so that it may be of benefit to yourself and others

Begin the meditation by letting your awareness descend into the body, right down to the ground, noticing that contact with the cushion, floor, or chair. Then let your awareness fill the whole space of the body. Be careful not to simply visualise or imagine the body, but simply witness the body. Naturally attending to the sensations that arise throughout this whole field of sensations.

As you mindfully attend to the sensations throughout the body, soften and relax those areas that feel tight, and especially with every outbreath, relax more and more deeply.

Once the body is relaxed and settled in its natural state, then settle your respiration in its natural rhythm. Utterly release with every outbreath, relaxing in the body, and happily letting go of any thoughts that might arise.

Then, following this same sequence, settle your mind in its natural state, giving up, for the time being, all concerns, hopes, and fears. Let the past remain in the past. Let the future remain unknown. Let your awareness come to rest in ease in the present moment, with stillness and natural clarity.

Now more narrowly focus your attention by directing it downwards to the rise and fall of the abdomen with each in and outbreath. In a very relaxed way, just notice the belly rise and fall with each in and outbreath. For some, it can be helpful to place a hand on the belly for a short while to locate these sensations.

Continue to let the breath flow effortlessly, without any intervention, and keep the muscles around the belly loose and relaxed. If you're sitting up, you might raise your sternum slightly, so that the belly can expand freely with each inhalation.

In time, make sure to use your faculty of introspection, monitoring your body, posture, breathing, and the flow of mindfulness itself. Recognise as swiftly as possible when excitation or laxity has set in and take appropriate action and restore your mindfulness.

To help balance the flow of our attention, we can draw from the pith instructions of Padmasambhava: each time the breath flows in, let this be an occasion for arousing and concentrating your awareness and pay very close attention to the inbreath. When the breath naturally flows out, let this be an opportunity for relaxing as you have never relaxed before. Relax your body, and release any thoughts that have arisen, while sustaining mindfulness of the sensations in the abdomen. With this gentle alternation of focusing in and then relaxing, you ward off both the excitation and laxity of the mind. Breath by breath, balance the flow of your attention.

Then, to help further calm this obsessively discursive mind and cultivate stability and continuity of attention, experiment with counting the breaths. Here, we replace many wandering thoughts with just a few regular thoughts of counting the breaths. At the very end of the inbreath, just before the exhalation begins, mentally, very briefly, count one. Then, at the very end of the next inhalation, count two. Don't let the count drag on through the breath, let it be a punctuation mark with each cycle of respiration. Let each count serve as a reminder to focus once again on the sensations of the abdomen. Count in this way, one through to seven, one through to seven, over and over, as long as it is helpful.

Before closing the meditation, dedicate the positive energy or merit that you've generated to your highest aspirations and intentions. Close with a few words of loving-kindness and compassion, such as "May all beings find happiness and the causes of happiness. May all beings be free of suffering and the causes of suffering".

4 - Mindful Activities

Mindfulness is about cultivating healthier ways to interact with the world, others, and our own thoughts, so that we can have more mental balance, more emotional freedom, and in doing so, we realise a calmer, happier life. With mindfulness, we gradually start to reduce and remove the tight, rigid, stressed mind which struggles so much in the modern world and cultivate a more open, present-centred, realistic, and creative mind. This mind is able to ride the waves of the highs and lows without so much of the push and the pull, the grasping at this and wanting more of this, the rejection of that and wanting none of that.

What is Mindful Movement?

Our fourth way of bringing mindfulness into our daily life is mindful movement. Examples of mindful movement are mindful eating or mindful walking. The point of mindful movement is to utilise our everyday activities like walking, eating, moving about, cleaning the house – whatever it is – as mindfulness practices. We do this by becoming more aware of the body, especially the sensations of earth, air, fire, water, and space within the tactile space of the body, but also the experience of the body in its immediate environment, the sounds, smells, visual impressions, and interactions with other phenomena. By tuning into our environment and the sensations in our body as we go about specific activities of our day, we'll bring ourselves back to the present moment and back to our baseline of peace and calm. Mindful movement helps the body and the mind to slow down and brings a calmer presence to our day.

Normally, we wolf down our food while scrolling on our phone, reading, or watching something on the TV, or we quickly eat something while managing the housework, work tasks, or kids. We might get halfway through our meal or even finish it before we realise we were even eating! We might say afterwards, "That was nice, I'm really full", but how do we really know it was nice? It just disappeared. The only thing left is a residual taste and a feeling from the body that says we should have stopped a couple of mouthfuls ago.

We may go about our day on autopilot with a quick pace, running around the house doing this, doing that, cleaning that, juggling this, organising that. As we try to do all these things at once, spinning all these plates, we fragment our attention as it flits between things quickly and this increases the pace of the mind, the pace of our thoughts, and leads to stress and burnout. Oftentimes, our way of being needn't be quite so fast. Unless we're cleaning and trying to increase our heart rate and keep the body healthy and moving, in which case it's of course very helpful, ordinarily there's no need to move around the house quite so fast. We may recognise these days where we get ourselves quite worked up, tense, stressed, hot, and bothered, and all we've done is make dinner for our family!

Mindful movement is about bringing awareness to more and more activities in our day and is especially recommended for those who find it hard to concentrate and for those who find it difficult to switch off. Research has shown that focusing on the present moment through mindful movement can help boost our wellbeing and our concentration and give the mind a break from trying to juggle so many different tasks at once. Mindful movement is a key practice found in Mindfulness-Based Cognitive Therapy because it helps improve our attentional skills, that is to say, our mind's ability to focus and concentrate. This particular benefit is among the many benefits that are gained through a mindful way of life that we've discussed previously in this book.

We Need to Take It Easy Sometimes

The simple objective here is to connect the mind with the body, and instead of just being busy with the trials and tribulations of daily life and getting through the day on autopilot, bringing mind and body into sync.

Our modern lives are like living with hundreds of windows and tabs open on our computer. If your computer was continuously left with loads of tabs open and we were opening new tabs all the time, then it would eventually crash. If you opened a program that was particularly resource heavy and the fan was running hot, the computer would need all the resource it could get and would struggle to perform efficiently with all these other tabs open. Our mind and our brains are the same. They need time out in order to reboot from time to time, to do some of the background processing, to give the fan a break, and we need to distribute our resource efficiently. To handle particularly challenging times in our life we may need a lot of mental power, a lot of creativity, and a lot of openness. When things really go wrong, and life is flipped on its head, we need all the resource, openness, calm, and inner strength that we can muster. We can't do that if we have tons of tabs open and we're trying to multitask so many things at once on a daily basis. We've reached capacity, it feels like there's no space, and we struggle to handle difficulties.

Mindful presence teaches us how to restore a sense of balance, a sense of ease, and a sense of preparedness. This means that sometimes multitasking is not the healthiest thing for us. Research has shown that our brains are not nearly as good at handling multiple tasks as we like to think they are. In fact, some researchers suggest that multitasking can actually reduce productivity by as much as 40%. According to Buddhist psychology, in one moment of mind, which may be as brief as one millisecond, your attention can only be focused on one thing. While we have the illusion of focusing on multiple things at once, our attention is actually jumping rapidly from one sense field to another continuously, and the mind makes sense of all of this input, and this is how we experience reality. When we multitask, we're splitting our attention even further, and this has been found to not be very productive, and not very healthy for our body-mind system.

Mindful Movement Practices

I am now going to describe the practice of mindful walking and mindful eating, two common mindfulness practices. I would recommend reading through these instructions, remembering them, and then taking the time to practice them and experience the benefits for yourself. Once you're familiar with doing these two, you'll understand experientially what mindful movement is, how it works, how to focus your awareness, and what on, so that you can engage in this way independently with other activities in your life.

Mindful Eating

This is perhaps one of the most well known forms of mindfulness because it's been used many times. It is commonly found in weight loss programs, but the benefits to be gained reach far beyond our weight. Mindful eating is about focusing on what you're eating, the experience of it, and how you're eating it. You could use just a piece of chocolate, a sweet, or a piece of fruit to start with, before practising in this way with a full meal. There are a couple of optional steps before picking up this piece of food, which I believe enhance the practice tenfold. But these are optional. Firstly, before you decide what you're going to eat, take a moment to bring mindful presence to your body in the here and now. Listen to your body, and ask, what does the body need? Think about the variety of foods you could choose from. What food makes you salivate more? Take your time and choose one piece of what you would like to eat, something that would be particularly intriguing enough for engaging in this practice for the first time. Once you've chosen a piece of food, extend your mindful presence from the body and take a moment to understand the interconnectedness of how you ended up with this piece of food. Bring awareness to all the people who were involved in growing that food; the rain that came to feed the crop; the sun; the soil; all the nutrients coming together from the soil, which was there because of fertiliser; all of the people involved in the packaging and processing of that food; the transportation of that food from wherever it came. Not to mention the technology we use to process and package food; the people who maintain the roads; the people who maintain the vehicles; the people who invented and designed the vehicles that were used. All the countless people and things from the natural environment that came together in a perfect way. Each of these pieces of the puzzle was essential for this particular piece of food to end up here with you. I feel it brings richness to the practice to take a moment first to appreciate this vast interconnectedness and feel gratitude that we have access to this food and for all the circumstances that came together to make it happen. From here, we begin with the actual mindful eating practice.

We begin by focusing on every movement, moment to moment, as we move our arm, our hand, our fingers, towards the piece of food as we pick it up. There may even be movements elsewhere in the body during this process. For your first time, really move quite slowly and take your time, sensing all you can sense. In the sensed let there be just the sensed. Then, position it either in the palm of your hand or grasp it between your fingers. Imagine that you're seeing this food for the very first time as if you were from outer space or an isolated tribe, and this is your first encounter with this delicacy. Look at it as if we have never seen it before, explore every part of it; what are the visual impressions appearing to our eyes, what are the tactile sensations appearing to our hand and our fin-

gers. Get a feel for the texture, the way the light hits the surface, the shape, its weight. Is it hard, soft, smooth, or coarse? Then, notice any thoughts that are arising. Even those such as "why am I doing this?" or "can I eat it now?" Any sort of thoughts that come up, relevant or not relevant. Allow these thoughts to occur, but don't follow the referent and allow the mind to wander. Notice the thought and bring your awareness back to the piece of food in your hand. Take the piece of food and place it beneath your nose, notice any smell impressions that appear to your nose. Perhaps bring it to your ear and squeeze it, roll it around, listen for any sound impressions that appear to your ears. As you bring it to your mouth slowly, notice how the arm and hand know exactly where to go, and notice the movement of the arm and the hand. Notice any other movements in the body. Notice that at this point our mouth may be starting to water. Gently place it in your mouth and take a bite. At first, don't chew, just feel how it weighs on your tongue, its size, its temperature, its texture. Explore all these sensations in the mouth. Notice if the rhythm of your breath changes at any point as you intentionally bite down on the piece of *food. Notice does it go to one side of the mouth, or does it stay in the centre? What flavours are being re-leased? What new textures have appeared? Then chew slowly and notice the changing consistency of the food, any new flavours, new smells, textures. No-tice the sensations in the jaw, in the head, in the throat, as you chew. When you naturally feel the need to swallow, do so, and sense how it goes down your throat, into the stomach. Notice any residual pieces on the tongue and in the mouth, notice any feelings or taste that you have after you've eaten that piece of food. When you're ready, repeat the exercise with the next piece of food.*

Whether we engage in this practice with a piece of food or a full meal, we bring an encompassing quality of attention and awareness in the same way as described above. We appreciate where the food came from, and we slowly make our way through smells, sounds, textures, and all of these sensations that we experience in the body, not just from our movements but also from our mouth. Thoughts are bound to pop into the mind from time to time, and that's OK, they're not an enemy to the practice but we can let them occur and we can notice them. We don't need to try and reject them, but simply bring our attention back to the food, back to the sensations, because that's where we are choosing to place our focus.

Mindful Walking

Walking mindfulness is another very common form of mindfulness, and it's taught especially to those who suffer from depression, low mood, and anxiety because general movement and getting out and getting fresh air is very healthy and beneficial for those conditions, not to mention the benefits from the mindfulness practice itself. To begin with, you want to make sure that the space where you're going to walk is clear of any obstacles. If you're going to be inside, you should remove any shoes and make sure that your path is going to be clear. If you are outside, then of course you want to wear some light shoes that are comfortable, but not restrictive so that your feet feel trapped. Also here, you want to ensure your path is not going to be full of obstacles. Perhaps doing this on a busy day in the city is not ideal if you need to stop and look around a lot as that's going to be quite distracting. Begin somewhere where it's going to be relatively quiet; a path along a lake or in the park, somewhere you would be able to walk ten or more steps before you're required to turn or stop for any reason.

Begin in the standing position, before you have started to walk, and notice how still your body is in that position. Feel your body's connection to the earth element - where you're in contact with the ground or the floor. Become aware of your immediate surroundings through our five senses: what you can see, what you can smell, what you can hear, what you can touch and anything you can taste. Take your time going through these five senses one by one, really bringing yourself to that experience of standing there in that position. Notice any thoughts and emotions that are present. Let them arise and let them pass. Notice where your arms are; you can hold them in front of you, hands together, to your side, or behind you. Wherever your arms are, just notice how they feel. Take notice of your breathing, become aware of how the air moves in and out of the body. Don't change your breathing, just become aware of it as you're standing there. Once you feel completely immersed in and aware of your surroundings and fully present, you may begin moving. Take your first step by shifting your weight from your left leg and lifting your right foot up, moving it forward, and putting it back down on the ground. Then, shift the weight of your right leg, lift your left foot up, move it forward, and put it back on the ground. Slowly, continue in this way, mindfully aware of all the sensations. Gently pay attention to the sensations on the bottom of your feet. As each part of your foot touches the ground, pay attention to how it feels; how we lift it, move it, place it. Notice your body's movements as you walk, your arms moving. Walking with full awareness. When it's time for you to turn or move around an obstacle, maintain that flow of mindfulness, and bring your awareness to the process of turning, paying special attention to each movement that you must do in order to turn yourself. Notice how your sides move. As you attend closely while you turn, you'll notice there are parts of the body that move that you don't even ordinarily realise. Then begin to walk *back to where you began. One step at a time, pay attention to how your feet feel, how your whole body feels. Naturally, you'll find a rhythm that you're comfortable with and balanced with. When you move forward, notice how your head feels, shoulders as well, how your arms and legs move at your side, or in front of you or behind you. Pay attention to your legs, your torso, your feet. Notice how they all work together to keep you in balance – automatically. You don't need to think about all these different movements, they just happen. Until I did mindful walking, I didn't even realise that when your left leg is moving, you shift your weight from the right to move it, and the same on the other side. I didn't realise all these different sensations and movements and different pieces of the body that are working together to keep you balanced, to keep you moving, without you having to think about it and pay attention to it. Thoughts are bound to arise during this practice, and when they do, allow them to come and allow them to go. Each time, returning your focus to the sensation of walking. As you walk, notice your breathing, notice how it has increased in rhythm. Again, there's no need to change it, just be aware of it.*

Continue to walk and practice for some minutes, and when you're ready, the next time you reach your starting place, just be still for a moment. Be aware of the sensations that are in the body as you return to stillness. Bring your awareness back to your breathing and notice the stillness as everything stops moving in the body. Finish by appreciating the time that you've spent here being mindful, and then move on with the rest of your day.

When you first do mindful walking, it's likely you will walk incredibly slow, and that's why I recommend people do this for the first time at home or in a private setting so that you can focus entirely on what you're doing and not on feeling out of place and self-conscious. As you become familiar with the practice, you'll find a rhythm that you're comfortable with, and it will become like second nature. Mindful walking is not something you'll do every time you walk as it is not always practical, but it is a very powerful way of bringing the mind back to the present and restoring balance when needed.

When To Practice Mindful Movement

These practices are very useful when we have time to do them. They're not a way of going about your whole day as there are times when it's not very practical. We can, however, bring this sort of awareness to any part of our day, not just eating or walking. Any movement can become a mindful movement. In particular, practices such as yoga or qigong. This helps us to reconnect with the quiet and calm of the mind and bring that balanced quality of present-centred awareness to our day.

We can actually train ourselves to automatically engage in mindful movement during specific tasks in our day, and many mindfulness practitioners do so. For example, every time you stand up could be an opportunity to become mindfully present again. Instead of just jolting yourself up and running off to make a cup of tea, you could instead move mindfully. First of all, notice how your body is seated or laying down currently, the weight of your body in whatever position it's in. Notice any sensations you're experiencing: vibration, tingling, throbbing, temperature, or any discomfort or tension. Let your awareness descend from the busy mind down into the body. Then, while paying close attention to the changing sensations and the movements of the body, gradually bring yourself to standing. Then, once you're standing, continue with your day as normal. Each time we have to stand up can be a quick opportunity to remind ourselves of the beauty of the present moment, particularly if we're regularly quite stressed or lost in thoughts about the past or future. It's a way of seasoning and complementing our day and bringing ourselves back, again and again. This is an invaluable skill and one which helps maintain our sense of inner calm and stops us from getting lost.

The practice of mindful movement is utterly simple. It begins and ends with a small step: bringing your awareness back to your body, your environment, and your actions in the here and now, and remaining there. You may find that as you engage in this practice more and more, something interesting happens. You may notice that the movement, the awareness, and the mind, merge – the mind holding nothing but the experience itself and that connection grows stronger. That experience is incredibly healing, soothing, and grounding. It's a very interesting experience that has ripple effects elsewhere in our life. It's the result of closing all of those tabs and windows on the computer. It's the process of putting all of the multitasking, organising, and thinking down for a short time, and every time we bring our awareness back to our body, it is like closing all of those tabs and just leaving the one open. That is healing and refreshing, and very helpful for our wellbeing.

Guided Meditation: Grounding through Body Awareness 🎧

To complement our look into mindful movement, I wanted to introduce an alternative practice to the present-centring practice we did earlier. Whenever we bring our awareness into the body, we ground ourselves in the present moment, because the moment we attend to the body or the breath, we are in the present moment. We cannot attend to the breath five minutes ago, or in five minutes' time. The same is true of the sensations of the body, there is only the here and now.

Take a moment to sit comfortably. Settle into the seven-point meditation posture. Bring to mind your most meaningful aspiration for this practice so that it may be of benefit to yourself and others.

Bring your awareness into the body, close your eyes, and breathe gently, quietly, slowly in and out through your nose.

With every exhale, allow the weight of your body to release further down towards the ground. Release the shoulders, hips, and legs towards the ground. With every inhale, notice an opposing upward lifting energy that lengthens your spine a little bit taller. Feel a gentle lightness, a gentle upward lifting.

Find a balance between these two breaths, grounding on the exhale, upward lifting on the inhale, and rest here for a while, feeling what it is like to sit in this way.

Focus your attention on the exhalation. Let each exhalation take a little more time than the breath in.

Lengthen and extend the exhale gently and comfortably, without trying too hard or pushing too far. Notice how extending the exhales in this way soothes and deepens your sense of relaxation.

Notice all the points of your body that are touching down and connecting to the ground below you, to the earth. This may be the soles of your feet, your ankles, your shins, the sides of your thighs. With every outbreath, as you further ground yourself by releasing energy down into the earth, imagine that each of these connection points expands and widens a tiny bit, just like a drop of water spreading on a surface.

Rest in ease, aware of this connection between the solidity of your body and the firmness of the earth.

When you notice the mind wandering, do not worry, this is natural. Without hesitation and without judgement, very simply, very gently, bring the mind back to the body. Check back in with your sense of the weight of the body, the form of the body, the solidity of the body.

Become curious about your sense of the body. Is it heavy or light? Still or in motion? Solid or fluid? Be present with the body, right here, right now.

The body can be an anchor for the mind. No matter where the mind goes, the body remains grounded. When the mind becomes turbulent, it has the grounded body to return to. Not just in meditation, but in daily life, when the mind runs away from you and thoughts are seemingly unstoppable, your body can be your anchor.

Before closing the meditation, dedicate the positive energy or merit that you've generated to your highest aspirations and intentions. Close with a few words of loving-kindness and compassion, such as "May all beings find happiness and the causes of happiness. May all beings be free of suffering and the causes of suffering".

Using Mindfulness of the Body to Heal Emotions

This meditation is especially effective when we get caught up in emotions and thoughts that we can't seem to control, whether that is thoughts of worry or guilt, or emotions such as stress, anxiety, or anger.

If we want to, we can take this meditation one step further. The body is a way for us to explore and heal difficult emotions. To do this, as you maintain a mindful presence in the body, bring your awareness to wherever you are experiencing the emotion, for example, a tightness in the heart or a knot in the stomach. Without pushing the emotion away and running away from it, instead attend to that sensation and allow it to be. After some time, gently ask yourself "What's going on here? What's the story hiding underneath this feeling, this sensation in the body?" Without trying to conceptualise your way out of it, attend to the sensation with a curious, attentive, and kind-hearted mood – as if listening to a grieving friend. Listen and see what comes up, rather than leading the conversation. By grounding yourself in the present moment and attending to the physical manifestation of your emotions quietly – calmly and with kindness – you move away from the doing mind which is trying to think its way out of problems and move into the being mind. The being mind has greater access to creativity, problem solving, and the openness required to work with our emotions. We may not feel the need to investigate the feeling itself right there and then, but by simply being present with the feeling itself, accepting it, and observing it moment to moment, we may find that the emotion releases itself, starts to dissipate and lose its power. This is an incredibly meaningful and resilient way to attend to our challenging emotions. Ordinarily, destructive emotional energy comes straight out in the form of harsh words or a tight fist. This is disempowering, and not a sign of strength but a sign of weakness. Being able to cooperate with our emotions and listen to them like a kind friend takes strength and courage, but it builds greater resilience, emotional balance, and results in greater peace of mind and happiness in life. We will look at a more structured version of this practice later in the section on Dealing with Destructive Emotions using R.A.I.N.

Questions and Responses

Question: Do you think it's helpful to bring mindful movement into our yoga practice?

Response: Absolutely! Yoga, qigong, tai chi, pilates, all these practices are opportunities to bring mindfulness to our bodies, helping us be present, lower stress, increase our energy levels, and strengthen that mind-body connection. I think having some sort of mindful movement practice is important for those of us who like to meditate and cultivate the mind. Whether that is just mindful walking or something like yoga or qigong. It's important to move the body, isn't it? And it benefits our meditation practice in many ways; mindful movement cultivates a calm mind but also releases any stagnant energies and stretches out any discomfort, stiffness, or tension we get from meditating for long periods.

Question: I like this analogy of the computer and all the tabs open. It's made me think about how busy I really am, and the importance of closing some of these tabs.

Response: You're right. It is important to close some of these tabs. I think many of us look to meditation and mindfulness to help us cope with really busy lives, in the same way someone might take a drug to help them do more and achieve more and be faster and more focused. The conclusion we come to is that eventually, this is a crash and burn technique. We're smothering not only our peace of mind but our creativity, problem solving, and intuition. Sure, meditation will really help us cope with a busy daily life, but actually, we need to bring awareness to the ways in which we treat our minds on a daily basis. Am I doing things that are healthy or harmful for my mind? Should I be simplifying some things and closing some tabs? If we truly want wellbeing and peace of mind, if that is important to us, then we need to ask ourselves these kinds of questions. The truth is that most of us are doing far too much!

Question: I struggle a lot with anxiety, I'm always catastrophising and coming up with worst-case scenarios. It seems I can't get my mind to stop, I'm always being tormented. How does this mindfulness and meditation help with that?

Response: This is such a common experience, and there are several ways that meditation helps with anxiety and worry. Do you have a meditation practice?

Question: I try, I do it sometimes.   _____

Response: And when you do, do you notice a difference afterwards?

Question: I do, I feel calmer, and my partner always says that I'm completely different, and he can always tell when I've done a meditation.

Response: Exactly! So, firstly, meditation is a way to get some relief, it is a way of giving us a break from the anxious thoughts. When you practice one of these methods we've talked about this week, or any meditation on the breath and so on, then we bring our awareness away from our mind and into the body. So, we're actively letting go of the worried thoughts by leaving them behind and focusing elsewhere. This gives us some relief and a chance for our body and mind to relax. So, it works well as a reset button and a way of self-soothing.

Question: But then it always seems to come back, it doesn't go away forever.

Response: And this is where we look to the second way that meditation helps us with anxiety, and these are the meditation practices that help us gain insight and get to the root of our anxiety. Anxiety and worry are fear based; they're based in uncertainty. By turning to our mind and our emotions, we start to gain insight into the nature of thoughts themselves and the stories we're being told by our mind. We start to become aware of how they function. With awareness, we find that we're able to influence them. So, we look at the mind and ask, "what is a thought?" "How do they work?" "Do I have to think every thought that comes up?" We learn to separate ourselves from the thoughts that arise. It changes from, "I'm anxious" to "there are anxious thoughts in my mind". And this distinction and different way of viewing anxiety is powerful. Normally, we believe every anxious thought. Every catastrophic outcome that we think of we completely believe. With some more awareness, we're able to stop buying into it so much. These thoughts lose their control over us, and we start gaining control over our mind. It starts with becoming aware of how it all works. It's a great question you've asked, and luckily, our next session is on this very topic – mindfulness of the mind, thoughts, and emotions!

Meditation Skills:
Enhancing Clarity

The third of three qualities that we're trying to cultivate, the apex of our pyramid, is clarity and vividness.

Clarity is all about how explicit and distinct our object of meditation is. It can be likened to going from a very blurry video to a high definition screen at maximum quality. As previously discussed, it is important that we enhance clarity without losing our continuity of attention or our foundation of relaxation.

We move now onto a third way of practising mindfulness of breathing which is classically taught in Theravada Buddhism. In this version, we bring our focus up to the sensation of the air at the nostrils.

This method has been around for many centuries and for extremely good reason, mostly its ability to help us cultivate clarity. When we're attending to the abdomen or the body, we attend to muscles moving up and down. But, here in this meditation, we attend to the actual air itself, either on the upper lip or at the apertures of the nostrils, wherever we sense it most.

This was the very first method of meditation I was introduced to and having practised it myself and heard a lot about this practice from others, from people who've come along to classes, and from my teachers, especially Lama Alan, the primary obstacle for many people is tension and headaches.

There's a danger that when we engage in this version of mindfulness of breathing we contract and become tight, especially around the eyes. With furrowed eyebrows and intense effort, we can develop a mild headache in the forehead. At this point, many decide to push through - "no pain, no gain". This headache then becomes chronic and can lead to tension elsewhere in the body. If this happens, then it's not long before you'll give up on meditation altogether and any enthusiasm for practice will dissipate.

This, however, is an avoidable problem. My teacher advised me that first of all, we shouldn't practice this mode with the air at the nostrils too early in our practice unless we have cultivated enough relaxation. When we do advance to this method, the advice, with very strong emphasis, is to keep our eyes completely disengaged from the practice. Avoid trying to focus the eyes down to the nostrils; avoid doing anything with your visual attention. Don't contract any of the muscles around the eyes. Don't focus your eyes on the tip of the nose or anything around the tip of the nose. All of that is the furrowing of the brow and intense focus, which gives rise to tension.

This practice is subtler than the version where we focus on the rise and fall of the abdomen. The sensations there are a lot coarser and more obvious. There are a lot of muscles going up and down, so it's easier, and that's why it is very good for cultivating stability of attention. However, if we're focusing on the sensations of the abdomen, we're not going to cultivate much clarity because it is quite easy.

Remember, our foundation is relaxation – getting ourselves to a point of being really at ease, relaxed, and comfortable. From there we build our stability, so that our meditation can carry on for longer periods of time without us losing focus and becoming uncomfortable. Then, this practice of observing the sensations of the air at the nostrils is very good for enhancing the vividness, which is our third quality we're trying to cultivate. The idea is that we're turning up to full definition, HD, 4K observation of the breath. This particular approach at the nostrils is very good for that, which later translates to us being able to concentrate better and have a better quality of attention in our daily life.

Another comment to make about what makes this practice unique is that the more you progress in the practice, the subtler the sensations become because your breath is becoming more and more subtle as your body settles. If you remain engaged with those sensations as they become more subtle, the vividness will increase as you need to attend closer. What you'll notice is that as the whole system begins to calm down, the vividness arises synergistically with that deeper sense of calm, quiet, and relaxation. This is an excellent sign that we're making progress.

Guided Meditation: Mindfulness of Breathing – Focus on Clarity 🎧

Take a moment to find a comfortable posture. Just as before, let your awareness descend into and fill the space of the body. Settle your body in its natural state, relaxed, still, and vigilant.

As you attend to the sensations in the body, relaxing and releasing any tension, let your breathing come and settle in its own natural rhythm, as if you were falling fast asleep. Let the body breathe without constraint.

For a short while, in a very soothing mode, strike the first balance of relaxation and clarity. Breath by breath, relax with every exhalation, relaxing in the body, and releasing troublesome thoughts. Breath by breath, settling into a deeper, deeper state of relaxation, but do not lose the initial clarity with which you began.

Check up on the muscles of the face, especially those around the eyes and the forehead, see that your eyes feel soft.

When you feel at ease, more narrowly focus your attention, without altering the breath, on the tactile sensations of the passage of air at the nostrils as you breathe in and as you breathe out. Take a moment to locate that area where you feel the sensation most.

Once detected, focus your attention single-pointedly on that target area. Remember that this is not about visualising the nostrils or directing your gaze downwards. Simply attend to the sensations of air as you breathe in and breathe out.

Continue to relax deeply, utterly letting go of the breath with every exhalation, and as you breathe in, arouse, and focus your attention, observing very closely.

Let your awareness be filled from moment to moment with this ongoing flow of tactile sensations of the passage of the breath. So continuous that there is no space for wandering thoughts to invade your attention.

Experiment with counting if you find it helpful. A brief count at the end of the inhalation, and apart from that, see if you can allow your mind to be as conceptually silent as possible.

In addition to the cultivation and refinement of mindfulness, also cultivate and refine the faculty of introspection. Now and again, monitor your posture, check that you're not restricting the breath in any way, and check the flow of mindfulness itself. As soon as you recognise that the mind has become distracted, remember what to do. First of all, gently relax, then release whatever has captivated your attention, and return to the meditative object. If you notice that you're becoming somewhat vague or spaced out, then take a fresh interest in the practice, and arouse and focus your attention.

When you feel that your body is quite relaxed and your meditation is stable, then start to enhance your vividness. Can you focus and attend so closely that even between breaths, you still sense some subtle movement of energy and air? Does it ever really stop and start again? Can you sense that the air appears to be warmer when you breathe out, cooler when you breathe in? Attend so closely to the passage of the air that you can sense these nuances, these finer details.

Release your narrow focus and bring your attention once again to the body. Before closing the meditation, dedicate the positive energy or merit that you've generated to your highest aspirations and intentions. Close with a few words of loving-kindness and compassion, such as "May all beings find happiness and the causes of happiness. May all beings be free of suffering and the causes of suffering".

5 - Mindfulness of the Mind, Thoughts and Emotions

The final of our five ways to bring mindfulness into our daily life is mindfulness of the mind, thoughts, and emotions. If you have been taking the time to engage in the previous practices over the time of reading this book, then you will surely have started to see for yourself how they bring a much more balanced, calm, and healthy approach to life. Of course, we still experience some ups and downs, and things in life will go wrong for sure, but with these five methods, we find that we're far better equipped, more resilient, and have greater inner strength to call upon. With familiarisation comes the ability to stay present-centred when things go wrong, with a more realistic and open perspective, rather than a very constricted, narrow view. With practice also comes access to patience, inner serenity, and the confidence in ourselves that we can deal with the trials and tribulations of daily life.

Each one of the practices I have introduced has its benefits and provides us with greater wellbeing. But as we see all of these practices coming together beautifully like a symphony, they make a mindful way of life. We start our day with a meditation practice, taking the time to get in touch with a relaxed, calm, focused state of mind and establishing our baseline for the day. With that foundation, we remind ourselves of our most meaningful aspirations for life so that as we go about our day, we make consistent choices that push us in that direction. We sprinkle our day with some mindful movement, mindful eating, bringing our awareness back into the body again and again, so that we maintain some connection with the present moment, and not so wrapped up in the future or the past, but on the here and now.

This final practice is the melody that brings our symphony together. In my opinion, this is the most important one of all. There is incredible potential to be discovered by becoming aware of the mind and mental events, coming to understand their true nature and discovering that we do not have to believe and follow every thought, memory, or emotion that pops up, but that we can exercise choice in which thoughts we pay attention to and which ones we let go of.

This is an essential life skill that we should have been taught from early childhood. It is by way of our thoughts, emotions, and mind that we experience reality. We all experience a similar physical reality, but each one is flavoured differently – by our mood, our beliefs, our thoughts, our state of mind, and so on.

By cultivating self-awareness of our thoughts, emotions, and inner workings of the mind, we become more aware of the relationship between awareness, our mind, thoughts, and emotions.

We Identify with Whatever Comes Up

Ordinarily, when a thought comes up in the mind, or an emotion comes up, we're taken and kidnapped by habits of the mind as we instantly latch onto it and identify with it. For example, when some sadness comes up in the mind, a feeling of being low, instantly we think or say "I am sad". It's as if "I *equals* sad". We attach our very identity, our very "I" and self to the emotion. Our whole experience has become one word, "sad", and we're thoroughly attached to it. When worrying thoughts come up in the mind, just like any thoughts, then instantly arises the notion "I am worried". In that moment, our whole experience and our whole being is worried; it's not just a worried thought. Self-awareness is all about getting to know how these thoughts arise, and in doing so, we can start to change our relationship with them. We can start to see that while thoughts arise, they are not "me". We can see that thoughts are not always meaningful, wise, and true – they are an option that our mind presents, and no more than simply a mental event arising in the vast space of mind. When we come to know that for ourselves experientially, it brings real freedom to our daily life. When we can detach ourselves from unhelpful thoughts and destructive emotions, then we can change everything.

Our whole experience can be influenced by our new-found capabilities and understanding.

There's a common misconception about meditation that it's all about clearing the mind of thoughts and getting to a point where you have no thoughts. This is not quite a correct view. In certain meditations, like the mindfulness of breathing practices described in this book, thoughts are definitely a distraction because they take you away from the object. But the thoughts themselves are not the issue; it's our relationship with our thoughts. In the mindfulness of breathing practice, we're not actively trying to get rid of thoughts by picking them up and throwing them away, rather we're just trying to, instead, choose to place our focus elsewhere. It's not about pushing them away, but about letting them pass by in the space of the mind, without going, "Ooh, what's that? Ooh, what do you want? Ooh, where are you taking me?" It's choosing not to follow along, but letting them arise, letting them pass, and choosing not to engage because we've decided to focus on something else. Ideally, we're not even trying to have a preference to have thoughts or not. If frustrations arise such as "I wish these thoughts would just go away", or, "I'm so distracted. Why am I so distracted?" we should recognise that these are also thoughts. We should also allow these thoughts to be and let them pass by. If they're particularly obsessive, often noting them can help – let the thought know you've seen it, note it and then let it go. Hold no preferences or expectations on how our meditation should or shouldn't turn out.

Most of Us Are Doing Far Too Much

Mindfulness of breathing is a really simple practice in actuality. It can seem very complicated sometimes, with all the tools and techniques to train our attention. But at its core, it's about focusing on one thing and letting all other things, including thoughts, fade into the background. In the same way that birdsong fades into the background, or the clicking of your mouse and your keyboard fades when you're working. This is not easy at first, especially with thoughts, because of our attachment to them and our habit of identifying with them. We have decades worth of training in using our mind the way that we do, and generally, we do too much. We're too busy not only juggling home, kids, work, but in our downtime, we add more stimulus: TV, music, or whatever. Some of the things that we fill our mind with may be enjoyable and bring pleasure, but to the mind, it's all the same: extra noise. That is why we can feel mentally exhausted even from enjoyable hobbies.

The mind is juggling all of our activities, responsibilities, lists, issues, and more, like a person spinning plates at the circus trying to manage each plate without losing balance. When we try to meditate and bring our attention to one thing, such as the breath, and rest there in stillness, it's like we said previously: giving a child tons of sugar, really hype them up and then ask them to sit quietly. What were we expecting? For many, normal day-to-day life is too busy, we're trying to do far too much; we're asking the mind to juggle far too much. This way of being is fine if we want to have a very uptight way of life and carry stress and tension around with us. But if we want to slow down, if we want some peace of mind, if we want to be able to meditate well, then we need to not just look at the way our mind acts in meditation, but look at the day-to-day, the thinking mind; how are we treating our mind? Is what I'm doing on a day-to-day basis resulting in a very overly active mind? For many, the thinking mind is on overdrive, constantly working things out, trying to figure things out, solve this, solve that, and our natural intuition and innate wisdom, that creativity, problem solving, is actually being buried by all of the turbulence of the thinking mind. Intuition, wisdom, creativity, and problem solving are accessed when the mind is calm, when it is clear, and we can experience that for ourselves.

Becoming Aware of Our Thoughts

As we practice meditation, over time, we start to become really aware of our thoughts, and the chattering mind starts to loosen its hold on us. Right now, every thought that comes up is taken to be meaningful, relevant, wise, and true, but, often, our thoughts are actually not very meaningful, not very relevant to what is actually happening, not wise, and sometimes not based on reality. Thoughts can be pesky little things. While we take each one seriously, some are definitely not to be trusted. For example, we can be in a group setting, either in a work meeting or with friends, and perhaps someone doesn't laugh at what we say or seems to pull a funny face at us. Then the thought pops up "they don't like you". Where did that come from? Then comes another: "that's why they avoid you, or that's why they do this, or that", followed by another, "it's because you're so egotistical, it's because you're so boring, no one likes you really". It can go on and on like this for a while, each thought popping up getting more and more off-topic and unhelpful. The first thing to acknowledge is not every thought is meaningful, wise, and to be believed. One of the first things we come to discover experientially when mindfully attending to the mind is that our thoughts – like everything – are actually impermanent. Thoughts can feel very real, solid, unchanging, and immovable. But actually, our thoughts are fleeting, and they are insubstantial. Thoughts also don't have a shape, size, or colour. They have no form at all because they are formless. This sounds obvious, but it is an important point to contemplate; thoughts are simply mental events arising in the great, vast ocean of our mind, which is expansive. They are nothing more than that. They can seem very powerful, alluring, even controlling. In actuality, the only power they have is the power that we give them by focusing on them, going along for the ride, believing them, reinforcing the story, and identifying with them. This is how they gain power and influence. This reification is how we pour fuel on the fire. Most of this is habitual, but it is self-inflicted.

An example of this is when we're upset with somebody. Let's say somebody did or said something that upset us. Some people have a tendency to drag out the hurt, by ruminating on it, going over it again and again, and telling everyone, "You'll never guess what they did! You'll never guess..." We remind ourselves at random intervals through the day and night, "I just can't believe it. I can't believe what they did, can't believe what they said". There is a metaphor commonly taught in Buddhism about *the two arrows*.

It is said that any time we suffer misfortune, two arrows fly our way. The first arrow comes from the experience itself – the thing the person did or said that hurt us. This one, very rarely do we have a choice in experiencing, it's instinctual. The second arrow, however, is self-inflicted, and one that we strike ourselves with every time we relive that event through our uncontrolled rumination. It's important to come to understand our thoughts so that we can get distance and perspective. With insight into the nature of thoughts, our relationship with them changes and they lose their ability to allure and manipulate us. It is then us who is in control, not them.

Thought Buses

One great way of looking at this is the analogy of the *thought buses*. Imagine you're at a bus stop, waiting for the number ten to take you home. While waiting, the number five comes along going in the opposite direction, and you get on it. After a while, you realise you're headed in the wrong direction, and you get off the bus and wait again at the bus stop. Then, you get on another bus taking you in a totally different direction again, and you get to the end of the line, and you realise, "I'm in the wrong place!" You then get on another one, and another, and another. This is like what is going on with the mind with our thoughts. A thought bus arrives at the bus stop and, regardless of where it's headed, we just get on. Sometimes these thought buses take us somewhere nice, but other times it takes us to "Panic Station", "Anxiety City", or "Sad Town". Despite where they're going, we get on anyway, automatically, and without choice.

If we were able to remain calm at the bus stop of the present moment and check carefully the buses that pull up with discerning mindfulness, then we would not end up in some of these scary places. Over time as we practice meditation, and in particular meditations like the one described at the end of this chapter, we can start to do just this. When a thought bus arrives, we can take notice calmly, and with conative intelligence – the awareness of what leads to our own and others' wellbeing – we can make the decision to consciously get on, or let it pass by. This doesn't mean we'll never find ourselves in the midst of a worrying thought pattern, of course. From time to time we will end up on the wrong thought bus, but that's fine, because we'll be able to recognise it more swiftly, we'll be able to get off without drama, and rest once again in the present moment, without criticism, without self-judgement, but with patience and acceptance.

The meditation we'll do at the end of this chapter helps us to start to see the space of the mind, rather than only the thought. Sometimes thoughts can feel big and scary, but just like when we look at the sky, we can be aware of the blue expanse, or we can be focused on the clouds alone. When we're caught up in thoughts, emotions, memories, and other mental events, we see only the clouds. It's like there are only clouds; there is no sky. Things feel tight, heavy, restricted, and it's difficult to see any break in the thoughts – difficult to get the mind to be quiet. Here, in this meditation, we practice taking a birds-eye view, we take a step back and observe the space of the mind; the space in which these thoughts and other mental events arise and see the spaciousness that is there.

This practice helps us detach from our thoughts, and realise that we are not our thoughts, that our thoughts are simply events that arise in the mind. Like our memories and feelings, they arise in the mind but our awareness, like a sovereign on the throne watching the people in the throne room, is separate from the people in the room. Like the sky, the mind itself is separate from the clouds, but the clouds arise in the sky. This is a wonderful thing to get the experience of; it's very beneficial, very helpful.

We need to get a handle on our thoughts. The worst part is that we believe every thought. Some thoughts of low self-esteem, for example. A thought arises, turns into a feeling, a feeling of not being good enough, not being worthy, of not looking good, of not being wanted, of people not liking you. The tragic thing is that we believe that thought as it arises, and it turns into a feeling. All your friends and family can tell you, "No, you look great! You look amazing! People love being around you! You're the life and soul of the party!" But we don't believe them. We don't believe it when they tell us, no matter how many people tell us, but, at the same time, we also want to hear it from them. This is the confused ego that is not really sure. You don't believe your family and friends, no matter how many people say it, but if one person reinforces it, if one person affirms that inner belief, then we are devastated. If we get the feeling that someone doesn't like the way we look, and they reject us or they avoid us, then we're devastated. The key thing here is we need to learn not to believe every thought that comes up. It's simply a thought. Venerable Robina Courtin calls it the *good roommates* and the *bad roommates* in the mind. The bad ones seem to be much larger, and they shout louder. We take more notice of the unhelpful thoughts or the bad roommates. No one ever says, "Oh, I just can't stop thinking good thoughts all day. All day, just good thoughts. Can't get rid of them!" It's always the negative ones that are the problem. The key point here is that we need to get to know our thoughts, so that we can hear them, and we can pause, and we can ask, "I wonder if this is true." Even just that simple question is very powerful and helps us to shift these difficult thoughts. To gain power over difficult thoughts, we need to get to know our thoughts on a daily basis, we need to pause, and ask, "is this thought meaningful? Is it wise? Is it true? Is it just one opinion, one mental event in the vast ocean of mind?" We need to have self-compassion for ourselves and stop believing it. Understand the reasons why they come up and how we can influence them. Is a thought really a thought if no one thinks it? Is it possible not to think a thought? Is it possible to observe a thought and not think it and not get on the thought bus? We'll see in meditation that this is very possible.

Thought Labelling

Another tool worth mentioning is thought labelling. When a negative thought appears in the mind it can have a lot of influence, for example thoughts of low self-esteem, when they appear in the mind, they feel like they have a lot of weight and influence. As we listen to it, we might not be able to disarm it by asking, "Is it true? Is it wise? Is it meaningful?" because we already believe it. What instead can be very beneficial is to label it. Even just as simple as "this is just a thought", for example. As a simple experiment, I'd like for you to come up with a negative thought right now that perhaps you regularly say to yourself. It needs to be negative, quite unhelpful, any negative thought about yourself that crops up in your mind from time to time. I want you to bring that thought to mind and repeat it to yourself quietly for about twenty seconds. Think of that thought and repeat it to yourself. What we can see from just artificially repeating this thought is that it has a bite to it, even if it's not coming from the side of mind but it's being artificially generated, it still cuts a bit and it's a little bit painful. Now, I want you to do that again, but instead, add the phrase, "this is just a thought", before it. For another twenty seconds, repeat the thought to yourself again, but each time add "this is just a thought". Even this little experiment can highlight quite a difference. This very simply phrase, "this is just a thought", helps us separate and detach ourselves from the referent of the thought. It reduces its pulling power. That is very helpful for us. Whenever I've introduced thought labelling, people have found it to be very beneficial if they're willing to give it a go. I encourage you next time that you are caught up in some negative thinking loop to try labelling the thoughts. Instead of rejecting the thought or trying to push it away or distract yourself – whatever we normally do – instead, pause. Try to get a feel for where it is in the body, all thoughts that have turned into emotions have a felt sense in the body as well, so try and get a feel for it in the body. Then, try to label the thoughts as they come in. If it's an emotion label, label it as an emotion. If it's a memory, label it as a memory. This detaches us. This gives us that bird's-eye view, that separation of our awareness and the thought, which normally become fused. In that separation, we can start to cultivate the ability to pause, to ask ourselves, "is this true?" Instead of believing the thoughts, getting on that thought bus wherever it's going to go, "Panic City", "Stress Station", instead, we can choose to jump off and say, "No thank you. This thought is not helpful. I don't have to believe this thought". Then, we choose to rest in the awareness of that felt sense in the body.

Dealing with Destructive Emotions

If emotions are particularly dominating, then we can take that initial awareness of the emotion in the body and use the R.A.I.N process. R.A.I.N. is a mindfulness tool that was designed as an "in the trenches" support for dealing with challenging emotions. It is an acronym for Recognise, Allow, Investigate and Non-Identification, or Natural Awareness.

Our first step is recognise. To begin, we try to recognise what emotion we are feeling and what it is that is going on. We could ask, "What is it that's going on inside of me right now?" Without leading the conversation or trying to grasp for an answer, we ask the question openly, feel the physical sensations and rest with it to see what comes up. As we identify the emotion, it can help to label it mentally or verbally.

Our second step, which happens immediately after recognition, is to allow or accept. At this point, we make an intention to allow that experience to be in the body, instead of immediately rejecting it or trying to get rid of it. This is about putting down the sword and shield and accepting that this is a part of our experience right now. We acknowledge that we have enough capacity in our heart and mind to allow the emotion and associated sensations to have its space. "There is space enough for you and me here. I do not have to fight you."

After we've recognised what it is that's going on and we've given it permission to be, we move onto the "I", which stands for investigate with kindness. We can begin by contemplating, "What is the story underneath this thought?", What am I believing?", "What is this emotion trying to tell me?" We do this with a sense of kindness towards ourselves, not judging ourselves for feeling this way, but understanding. It is crucial here that we continue to resist the urge to lead the conversation. The example I often give is like listening to a grieving friend. You don't talk at them, explain away their feelings, or expect them to be different or to not feel what they feel, instead you listen with kindness and let them talk and vent. In the same way, we attend to ourselves and inquire into this emotional experience. We ask the question and see what bubbles up. Many find this to be very insightful and powerful. If you have a very honest and trusting rela-

tionship with a partner or a loved one, this is something you could even do together. If you or they appear to be feeling stuck in an emotion and you're not
sure of where it's coming from, do the R.A.I.N process
out loud: "OK, where are you feeling it in the body?
What does it seem to be telling you?" You might
come up with something like, "I don't know, I just feel
unsettled" or "I think it's boredom", and then you can
say, "Well, what's underneath that boredom?" Perhaps
there's some feeling that your surroundings are not
good enough, some frustration at a supposed lack of
progress in life. What's underneath that? Perhaps a
belief that we're stuck, that we should be doing better. Perhaps this stems from a lack of self confidence.

Whether you do it alone or with a trusted other,
you may just uncover insights and beliefs that you
didn't know were there. Every bad thought, anxious
feeling or piece of distress has a cause. Nothing
arises without causes and conditions. And eventually,
we may find that it all comes down to ego or self-
cherishing. The ego wants something, the ego is unhappy. We're not getting what we want or we're having to experience something we don't want. We have

expectations that are being thwarted. Usually, you can find that it comes down to something like that.

Once the insights have come to light through our investigation, we may find that we feel better. Like listening to that grieving friend, once the snot and tears have come through, the emotional energy has been released. Then we come to the N which is natural awareness or non-identification. This is a natural crescendo of the R.A.I.N. process, you come to a recognition that this emotion and the associated thoughts and feelings are not you, that they are impermanent, and you can rest in a natural awareness of the present moment and any residual sensations in the body.

As we do this process, the uncomfortable energy of the emotion has the space to release itself. This is a comforting and insightful practice, and one which creates a very worthwhile alternative to slamming a door or saying harsh words, which can be common ways for the energy of destructive emotions to come out.

Observing the Mind, Thoughts, and Mental Events

The primary way that we gain control of our thoughts and feelings is by getting to know them and becoming familiar with the nature of our mind. What is the mind? We all know that we have a mind, and we can identify states of mind such as unhappy, happy, anxious, or confused. But do we know what the mind is, where it is, and how it functions? Many of us may point to our head or believe the mind to be the brain or some property of the brain. This is a common belief, but it is only a belief and not scientific fact. Upon closer investigation, we see that the mind is not the brain and cannot be. Firstly, one is matter and can be photographed, scanned, poked, and prodded. The other is formless, has no physical properties and cannot be photographed, scanned, poked, or prodded.

There is definitely a connection between the two; brain chemicals affect our state of mind, and states of mind affect brain chemicals and sensations in the body. However, correlation does not mean they are equal. When you flick on a light switch, the light comes on, when you flick the light switch off, the light goes off. The light switch is not the light. There is correlation, but no evidence to support they are one and the same. When you type on a keyboard or move a mouse, things move on the computer screen. Again, we understand that the keyboard is not the screen, and the screen is not the motherboard, storage drive and so on. While there is a default assumption that the mind is the brain – and many people use the words brain and mind interchangeably – that experiment was never done, and this has never been proven.

The nature of the mind is space and luminosity. It is a formless continuum without shape or colour. It is with the mind that we perceive, understand and remember. It has no boundary, it is not located inside the head or limited to the space of the body. If you sit on a mountain top and look over a really expansive landscape, you can observe something that is miles away and you can be aware of what it is you see. You can look up at the stars and observe phenomena an unfathomable distance away. These visual objects are arising in the space of the mind, in dependence upon your eye organs, visual cortex, and eye awareness. So, the mind cannot be confined to the head or the four walls of the room that you're in. When we understand or perceive something, we do so only because of our mind.

In Buddhism we often see the mind and thoughts introduced through the analogies of the sky and clouds, or the ocean and waves. The sky is a vast, blue expanse. It is clear and unobstructed. Just like thoughts form and dissolve in the mind, so do clouds form and disperse across the open sky. The sky does not crave one type of cloud over another, nor does it prefer to have clouds or not have clouds. The clouds simply pass through the space of the sky. Sometimes there are many clouds, sometimes it is stormy and there is a lot of turbulence and movement. Whatever the weather, the sky remains clear and expansive, and above the clouds it remains a blue clear space. Likewise with the mind, no matter how stormy, turbulent, or noisy the mind becomes with thoughts, emotions and other mental events, the space of the mind remains spacious and clear. It is within this spacious clarity that all mental events arise and dissolve.

Similarly, just as the waves of an ocean can be turbulent and choppy or relatively calm and still, so too the movements of the mind can be turbulent or relatively still. Either way, below the surface there remains a clear spaciousness which is calm and peaceful.

There is value in becoming more aware of the *space* of the mind and identifying with that rather than the thoughts themselves, and that is the aim of this next meditation. In this meditation we see the mind as like the sky, and our thoughts as like clouds. It is recommended for this meditation that you be seated upright, and that you leave your eyes naturally open.

Guided Meditation: Observing the Mind and Mental Events 🎧

Settle into a comfortable seated posture. For this practice, I recommend keeping your eyes open.

Take some time to settle your body in its natural state, imbued with the three qualities of relaxation, stillness, and vigilance. Deepen your relaxation with every outbreath. Enhance your stillness and your stability and remain vigilant.

To help settle the mind and bring it into a state of focus and concentration, ready to engage in the meditation, spend several minutes engaging in mindfulness of breathing.

When you gain a deeper level of focus, allow your mind to be attentive and observant of whatever comes to notice, regardless of what it is. Don't identify with any thoughts or feelings that arise, simply observe them. Almost like looking out of a window and watching people pass by. Without getting involved, simply allow all mental events to arise and pass by.

Imagine your mind as being just like the sky. Completely clear, vast, spacious, and without end. Concentrate on this experience, identify with this experience of clarity, spaciousness, and awareness.

See your mind as completely clear, just as the sky is completely clear. Sometimes clouds fill the sky and obscure the sunshine. But the sky doesn't become up-

set, nor does it identify with the clouds or judge the clouds. The clouds pass through the spaciousness of the sky – they come, and they go. The clarity and spaciousness of the sky aren't compromised by the clouds as they arise and pass.

When a thought, an emotion, an idea, or an image arises in your mind, just observe it. As if you would observe a cloud. Let it arise, and let it pass.

See every mental event as just like a cloud, and your mind like the sky. Concentrate on that experience of spaciousness.

Whenever we identify with and we're carried away by thoughts, we lose any awareness of this spacious clarity of our mind, and our perspective becomes small and constricted, as if all there was, was clouds.

But when we can simply observe these thoughts and feelings arising without getting involved, then we can identify with the sky instead of with the clouds. Then we can reside in the spacious purity that is our basic clarity of mind.

Focus on this calm, clear, peaceful, open spaciousness of mind – this space without agitation, without delusion, without anxiety.

Continue with this experience, simply observing these thoughts like clouds and your mind like the sky. In this meditation, there is nothing to do except to be aware and to allow your cloud-like thoughts to arise and pass by. See if it is possible for your awareness to remain still in the midst of this motion, observing without judging or following.

Before closing the meditation, dedicate the positive energy or merit that you've generated to your highest aspirations and intentions. Close with a few words of loving-kindness and compassion, such as "May all beings find happiness and the causes of happiness. May all beings be free of suffering and the causes of suffering".

Questions and Responses

Question: I really like the image of the clouds, you know, the sky. I found it very helpful to think of space, so I'm thinking the next time, which will probably be tomorrow when I wake up, the next time that I'm feeling anxious, I'm going to try that: actually picturing the sky with the clouds and creating more space between them.

Response: I'm glad that resonated with you. When I think of my own experience with anxiety, it – for me, I know it's different to everyone – but for me, it always felt very heavy. It felt like, almost like a dark cloud, it had quite a presence on me. And, yeah, in that moment, it's all you see, it's all you can think about, it's just this experience and nothing else. But taking that step back like you just said, seeing the sky mind as well, remembering that there is spaciousness, I can see how that would be really beneficial for that sort of experience, so let me know how it goes.

Question: Yeah. I was thinking when you said about the dark cloud, I think for me, it's more – it suffocates me. But I don't see it as dark, I just see it as overwhelming. Yeah, so the space and everything might work quite well. I should give it a go. Thank you.

Response: You're very welcome. That's the thing, we've got to give all these practices a go, to see what works for us, and hopefully we'll find our combination that comes together and works.

Question: I've missed a few sessions which has been a real shame – things have just a bit chaotic lately. But, yeah, tonight's been really good, and it's been really nice to get back into having that time to meditate and just having that time for myself. I didn't realise how much I missed it until I didn't have it. So, yeah, it's been really good.

Response: You're so right – you don't know you miss meditation until you stop, and also, it can be hard to get the motivation to meditate or to come and do a class, to listen to me waffle on for a bit and do some meditations. Motivation is a big thing. It's the same with the gym isn't it? And that's because we think of going to the gym as this stand-alone thing, a one hour experience which, on the face of it, isn't particularly pleasurable. What we forget is the bigger picture, why do I want to go to the gym in the first place? Why do I want to meditate? Don't think about the 20 minutes or so of meditation in isolation but think about what it means to you. What are your reasons why? "By meditating I feel calmer and I'm able to respond better to my family and my work. This means I have more harmony in my relationships and my job goes by easier. Because of this, I x, y and z." Consider your 50 reasons why, really solidify in your mind why it's important to you. Then it becomes a case not of "I should do it" but "I absolutely must do it!"

Question: Thank you for sharing that short experiment of repeating a negative thought with "this is just a thought" in front of it. I found that so interesting! I'm someone who really believes my thoughts, I follow the story all the way to the worst possible outcome. And this, I think, could help me step back from that; step off the bus.

Response: I'm so glad that you really felt that difference. For me too, personally, I notice that it really takes the sting out of it. It makes the thought less believable, and you start to question if it's really true. Beforehand, you believe it unconditionally, but now you begin to think "really?" and there's an element of disbelief. One of my teachers, Venerable Robina Courtin, often says that it's one thing that we have these negative thoughts, but the worst part still is that we buy into it and believe it. We really take it to be 100% absolute fact. That's the heartbreaking thing. So, these practices and ways of thinking we've explored today are all for the sake of taking that step back and not buying into it anymore. Thoughts are formless, temporary mental objects whose only power is the power we give to them. Let's hear that again: thoughts are formless, temporary mental objects whose only power is the power we give to them. Knowing this and understanding it is so empowering. Until now, we've had no choice. Our mind has been a mess and our reality has looked overwhelmingly negative, and we've been forced into that position. But now, we've been shown the tools to turn that around. Now we can take responsibility and stop believing the stories. It's not easy, not at all, but it's absolutely possible. And as Shantideva says: "it's impossible to cover the whole world with soft material to protect our feet, but wearing shoes is an option." It's impossible for us to fix the whole world, but it is possible for us to fix our own minds.

Meditation Skills:

Tips for Building a Daily Practice

When we think about building a daily meditation practice, the emphasis is right there on this word practice. It is a journey, and one that will have ups and downs along the way. The truth is that everybody's practice will look different. We all have different karma, predispositions, levels of enthusiasm, and motivations.

Building a daily habit of meditation is like building any other habit. It takes time, patience, and discipline, especially when it goes against any old habits we may have. Having said that, it needn't be something difficult. We build this new life changing habit one day at a time. There's no need for our practice to go one way or another, no need for change to feel quick or slow, and no need for it to resemble some imaginary feeling of inner peace.

Here are some suggestions that may help pave the way to establishing a daily practice. There are no hard and fast rules, and I recommend experimenting to see what works for you.

When should I meditate?

Many people prefer to meditate in the early morning, not long after they've woken up. At this time, the outer world is usually quieter, you're well rested, and your mind hasn't yet been shaken by the trials and tribulations of the day. Morning meditation can be a wonderful start to your day, and if combined with a contemplation of your aspirations, helps to set the tone for the day. If you'd like to try cultivating a morning habit, I'd recommend it to be the first thing you do – other than a shower or washing your face which can help to wake you up – and avoid checking your phone or activating yourself too much beforehand. If you feel you may not be able to fit it in to your morning schedule, consider waking up slightly earlier.

Other people find it easier to practice in the afternoon or at bedtime. No time is particularly better, it's about what suits your lifestyle and your psyche. However, try to plan ahead and practice at the same time every day as this is the best way to build a habit.

Where to meditate?

Establish a quiet and comfortable place for your daily practice. If you have the space, it could be somewhere that you designate for practice only. Over time, this space will have a calming effect on you and through association, you'll find it easier to settle into the practice. Even if you can't create a designated place, do try to pick somewhere where you will be undisturbed and where you can easily move your cushion or chair to and from. If it helps, make this space inviting and comfortable. Some people like to include things like soft furnishings, candles, incense, an inspiring book, or a statue of a Buddha. None of this is required of course, but rituals and symbols can be helpful for some.

How long to meditate?

Our emphasis should be on quality, not quantity. It is far better to have five minutes of meditation that goes well, than 40 minutes of frustration or sleep, which builds another bad habit. I recommend starting with one or two daily sessions of short duration, dictated by your level of enthusiasm and freshness before you begin. In the beginning this could be as little as one minute, or the counting of just seven breaths. For others, 15 or 20 minutes feels very doable – being not too short or too long – just enough time to get into the practice but not so long that we're lost in distraction. The main thing is that we have the resolve to show up at the same time every day, and we do so. Remember, you don't get the benefit of a meditation you do not do!

Another recommendation is to decide how long your practice will be before you settle into your posture, and to set a gentle timer for that length of time. This helps prevent discursive narration and uncertainty about how long you've been meditating and whether you can stop yet!

Good in the beginning, good in the middle, good in the end

The Buddha once said that his Dharma is "good in the beginning, good in the middle and good in the end". Our meditation practice should be the same. What this means is that we begin every meditation with enthusiasm and a meaningful motivation. Take the time to contemplate why you are meditating, and who are the beneficiaries of your practice. This really gives your practice some power and makes it a virtuous activity. Good in the middle means that we practice with freshness, and we focus well for the duration of the session. As I mentioned, let the length of your meditation be dictated by your level of enthusiasm and freshness, so that your practice is always good in the middle. Good in the end means that we finish our formal practice on a positive note. We should be feeling quite relaxed, not tense or frustrated, and we should take the time to dedicate the positive energy, or merit, that we've accumulated through our meditation practice to our highest aspirations. We can do this with a few simple lines such as, "Through the merit of my practice, may I achieve enlightenment for the sake of all sentient beings. May all beings find happiness and the causes of happiness. May all beings be free of suffering and the causes of suffering".

Integrating Mindfulness Into Our Daily Life

We've now explored five simple ways to restore presence and calm amidst challenge and change in daily life. As stated at the start of this book, all meditation practices and teachings of Buddhism are to be tested for ourselves. Should you put these methods into practice, then just like myself and many others before me, you may experience the benefits that mindful living can bring you. No matter who we are, by training the mind we are able to start living with greater ease, gracefully handling the ups and downs of human life. We may find that through this inner journey, our enthusiasm for the path of self-exploration and enlightenment naturally increases.

We may wonder what to do next? Firstly, I would encourage you to continue to use this book. Unlike reading a fiction novel, my hope is that this book is not a one-time read, but a practical guide that offers you something new each time you open it. To quote

Lama Alan: "although our memory may be reasonably good, we probably cannot recall everything that came up in the text". For mindfulness to become an integral part of our natural way of living, we need to go over these practices again and again and build new habits for daily living.

Alongside these mindfulness practices, remember the importance of the *Four Immeasurables*. The state of enlightenment has two wings: wisdom and compassion. As we actively cultivate mental balance and wisdom, we mustn't forget the equally important aspect of approaching ourselves and our fellow sentient beings with loving-kindness, compassion, empathetic joy, and equanimity. These practices open our hearts, ease our fears and counter any distortions in our relationship with ourselves and others.

Community is another important part of our path. Consider joining our online meditation and discussion groups or in-person retreats where you can practice with others and share your experience. Community can not only be a source of inspiration, but also an opportunity to share, learn from, and help others who are on a similar journey.

Next, if you wish to continue your journey beyond mindfulness and into the realm of the Buddhist path to awakening and enlightenment, I recommend that you find someone whom you can call your teacher. The Dalai Lama was once asked, "Does one need a guru in order to achieve enlightenment?" He thought for a moment and answered very carefully: "No, but it can save you a lot of time." The importance of having a skilled and compassionate teacher who can show us the path and help us proceed along it are widely emphasised in Buddhism, and for good reason. Not only for saving us time, but in making things clearer and dispelling doubt. Take your time with this, gaining experience with several teachers over long periods of time, investigating their teachings and checking out their students, until you are sure that this is someone whose values, knowledge, skills, and qualities of the heart radiate outwards, bringing the same out in you.

I hope this book has inspired you to take back control of your experiences and cultivate genuine happiness. We are each the authors of our own lives, and it is up to us and only us to bring about the lasting change we wish to see in ourselves and in our world.

It is my hope that one day we see a radical revolution in human society, one where we turn away from the endless pursuit of hedonic pleasure at the expense of our planet and its inhabitants, and towards values of the heart, inner peace, and harmony.